Judy Mathieson

MARINER'S COMPASS QUILTS

Setting a New Course

◆ New Process ◆ New Patterns ◆ New Projects

C&T PUBLISHING

Text and Artwork © 2005 Judy Mathieson

Artwork © 2005 C&T Publishing, Inc.

Publisher: Amy Marson

Editorial Director: Gailen Runge

Acquisitions Editor: Jan Grigsby

Editor: Darra Williamson

Technical Editors: Joyce Lytle and Carolyn Aune

Copyeditor/Proofreader: Wordfirm, Inc.

Cover Designer: Kristy K. Zacharias

Design Director/Book Designer: Rose Sheifer, Graphic Productions

Illustrators: Jack Mathieson, Micaela Carr, Donna Yuen, Richard Sheppard

Production Assistant: Kerry Graham

Photography: Sharon Risedorph and Luke Mulks, unless otherwise noted

Published by C&T Publishing, Inc., P.O. Box 1456, Lafayette, CA 94549

Front cover: **Pulsar With Drifting Geese Border** by the author

Back cover: **Twilight Star with Geese** (top only) and **Hawaiian Star**, both by the author

Title page photo: Rose Sheifer

Mathieson, Judy.
  Mariner's compass quilts : setting a new course : new process, new patterns, new projects / Judy Mathieson.
    p. cm.
  Includes bibliographical references and index.
  ISBN 1-57120-300-1 (paper trade : alk. paper)
  1. Quilting–Patterns. 2. Patchwork–Patterns. 3. Compass in art. I. Title.

TT835.M38824 2005
746.46'041–dc22   2004029491

Printed in China

10 9 8 7 6 5

Dedication

To all the quiltmakers past and present who were willing to take on the challenge of this classic design.

A special salute to all my students over the years, whose enthusiasm has helped me to learn along with them.

Acknowledgments

Thanks to my husband, Jack, who helped in all the preliminary technical aspects of this book and without whom the book would not have been possible.

Thanks to the staff members at *Quilter's Newsletter Magazine* for their encouragement.

Thanks to Christine and Neil Porter, whose connection with Bristol Cathedral in the UK made possible one of my favorite creations.

I hope you, the reader, enjoy the quilts of those who entrusted me with their own creations: Janyce Anderson, Joyce Balzley, Susan Cleveland, Jan Fitzhugh, Iris Frank, Carroll Griffiths, Linda Humphrey, Judy Jordan-Biesele, Gloria Kennedy, Lyric Kinard, Jan Krentz, Jetty Morton, Susan Rossi, Ann Shuken, Lynn Spurlock, Gerry Sweem, Jeanne Thomas, Maureen Thomas, Marianne Watada, and Betty Whitman.

The staff at C&T has been ever helpful. Special thanks to my editors, Darra Williamson and Joyce Lytle.

Fishy Star, 31" x 31", by the author, 2004

Contents

Foreword

I have been making Mariner's Compass and other circular star quilts since 1980, and it is still my favorite pattern. In 1987 I wrote a book titled *Mariner's Compass: An American Quilt Classic,* and in 1995 I updated my ideas in *Mariner's Compass Quilts: New Directions.* Here it is, ten years later, and I am still fascinated with the design.

Quiltmakers around the world are continually introduced to new patterns and creative ways of working with fabric, but many still enjoy the challenge of the radiating star. Part of the fascination has been—and no doubt remains—the technical challenge of sewing all those sharp points and still having a flat circle when the sewing is completed. Over the years, quiltmakers have enthusiastically adopted foundation techniques to get past some of the technical problems. In *New Directions,* I offered techniques that worked for me at the time; however, since then I have "evolved" and developed new techniques.

The number of quiltmakers is increasing every year, as the fabric industry produces more appealing cotton fabrics, as inventive people manufacture helpful tools, and as talented quiltmakers invent new, efficient techniques and publish exciting books to tell others about them. I hope this book provides some new designs and suggestions that you can use to make your quilts uniquely your own.

I have chosen not to cover the very basic quiltmaking techniques, since I think most people who are attracted to the Mariner's Compass pattern have more than beginner-level skills. (This also leaves more room for patterns.) A wealth of books covering all aspects of the quiltmaking art are available to you if you need them. The bibliography on page 95 lists several recommended basic books. If you can't locate these titles, ask for help at your local quilt shop or bookstore, or check the public library. Quilting periodicals carry advertisements for books, and there are companies that specialize in mail ordering books of interest to quiltmakers. If you are knowledgeable with a computer, the Internet represents a great resource too.

> Quiltmakers around the world are continually introduced to new patterns and creative ways of working with fabric, but many still enjoy the challenge of the radiating star.

Heron's Way, 24" x 38", by Maureen Thomas, Emsworth, UK, 2001

Introduction

Piecing the Mariner's Compass design requires precision, but you don't need to put it off forever just because someone once told you it was difficult. I often ask students at the beginning of a class if they have made a Mariner's Compass before. Those who have usually agree that it was much easier than they envisioned. So don't let others frighten you. Just start with a star that matches your skill level.

Here, in my third book on Mariner's Compass-style quilts, you'll find information on planning these quilts, with examples that range from traditional to innovative.

The chapter on drafting will guide you in easy steps through the process of designing your own patterns, if that is your wish. Basic drafting has not changed much since my previous books were published, but I have included new information on creating outer rings of points, circling geese, and expanding checkerboards that work with the basic stars. It isn't difficult to draw a star to your own taste or desired size, and once you get comfortable with the techniques, you can draft a star into any shape that suits your fancy, not just circles and ovals.

The chapter on fabric selection includes advice that is based on the experiences I have had in making my quilts and that I think you will find useful.

There are many construction techniques for making these designs. Since they require precision, I prefer to use foundation methods. The chapter on construction details my methods for using perforated freezer-paper foundations as well as regular paper foundations. Any traditional method of hand or machine piecing is still appropriate but will require separating the shapes in the foundations into separate templates.

For some time, quilters have been using paper templates to increase the accuracy of their results. Freezer paper—paper with a light plastic coating on one side—sticks to fabric when it is pressed with a heated iron. The paper can be used for traditional designs with multiples of the same shape, and it is particularly helpful with designs such as ovals and off-center stars, in which many of the pattern pieces are unique and used only once. Sewing directly through paper foundations that have been printed with segments of the pattern and then removing the paper can increase precision while sewing and the accuracy of the finished block. I have developed a fold-back method of using freezer paper that eliminates the process of tearing out the paper when the sewing is completed. You'll find this method discussed in the following pages.

The pattern section includes numerous examples of Mariner's Compass and radiating star variations that you can mix and match as you please in your quilts. The project section includes instructions for two quilts: a bed-sized quilt (*Kyoto Stars*) and a smaller wall quilt (*Pulsar*). You can use the same stars I used in these projects or substitute other star patterns of the same size. Also included is a pullout sheet with full-size patterns for the background blocks, a large 64-point star, two oval stars, and an expanding checkerboard pattern designed to fit a Mariner's Compass star with a 15-inch diameter.

The Mariner's Compass: History and Inspiration

Mariner's Compass is the name quilters use to refer to star designs that radiate from the center of a

24-Point Star, 86" x 86", maker unknown. In the collection of the author. This 24-point star design is not a Mariner's Compass.

circle as opposed to star designs that grow from a square, such as the Ohio Star. For your quilt to be called a Mariner's Compass quilt, the star should probably have 16 or 32 points—the same as the compass card on a magnetic compass.

During the sixteenth century, cartographers made wonderful sailing charts, letting their imaginations run free in the process. You can benefit from studying these beautiful charts for their use of color and symbolism. The wind rose came to be used with a lodestone to find the direction *north* in the magnetic compass. English-speaking countries call this emblem a compass rose. It is not clear exactly how the fleur-lde-lis came to represent north on the compass rose, but it was a motif used by the French monarchy, and many prominent cartographers of the time came from France.

An 18-point star decorates this tourist souvenir from Costa Rica.

This book contains several patterns for stars inspired by these nautical-style designs, along with some appliqué patterns for that companion design—the fleur-de-lis representing north—as well as the letters S, E, and W representing south, east, and west. While a star with a basic division of five would hardly be helpful in finding north, south, east, or west, a star with any number of points or outside configurations could certainly be called a Mariner's Star, since the stars in the night sky are also used to find direction.

A small wooden cart from Costa Rica with a 12-point star painted on the wheels

One of my favorite designs from *New Directions* is the 20-point Twilight Star. I have included this pattern once again (pages 76–79), but in two new sizes. There is also a circling geese pattern for Twilight Star, along with a number of new quilt examples.

In almost any culture, you can find design sources that use these central radiating designs. Among my favorites are the painted designs found on the wheels of carts in Central America, particularly in Costa Rica. These designs often use basic divisions of three or six and incorporate the six primary and secondary colors (red, yellow, blue, green, orange, and violet).

Large star designs are perfect for the center of symmetrical medallions, and oval designs add grace to any quilt. If you get an impulse to try something a little different, begin a round design off-center for a whole new look. The possibilities are endless.

Detail of wheel

Planning Your Quilt

Floor in Bristol Cathedral, Bristol, England. Photo by Neil Porter.

What inspires a person to make a quilt?

Detail of block from a 32-point star quilt, maker unknown, circa 1880. In the collection of the author.

What inspires a person to make a quilt? The need for bed covering, the desire to give one's work as a gift, or just the pleasure of working with special fabrics are all good reasons to make a quilt.

Whatever the reason that inspires you to make a quilt with radiating star designs, you'll soon discover that these patterns have special design challenges. How can I say this without sounding silly? These patterns are so circular and so spiky at the same time. How do you adapt them to make a quilt, which is usually some form of a square or rectangle?

I have been designing quilts using these stars for about twenty years. I have reached the point where almost everything that includes a circular space leads me to imagine how it would look as a star quilt. The floor of Bristol Cathedral, in Bristol, England, has lots of places to put stars and—in fact—already includes some. I was inspired to add more stars, simplify the background, and generally adapt the design into a quilt. John Pearson, the designer of this floor, had been inspired by a trip to Italy in the early 1900s.

Bristol Stars, 83" x 83", by the author, 1999

However, let us start closer to the tradition and look at some classic quilt solutions.

Placing a radiating star in a block can have two different results. The star itself claims the spotlight if the piecing wedges that hold the circle together are the same fabric or value as the background of the square.

If you choose fabric for the background square that is a different value than the wedges that hold the star together, you have a new design challenge: you have now added an obvious circle within the square, as demonstrated in *Royal Star* (right).

Inserting the star circle into a square and then setting it with horizontal/vertical sashings and corners squares is a classic way to feature an elaborate block. See *Kyoto Stars* (page 89) for an example.

Putting blocks on point always increases the energy of the quilt. Lynn Spurlock created a dynamite set with a variety of stars in different sizes in *Midnight Garden* (below).

Royal Star, 29" x 29",
by the author, 2000

Midnight Garden,
64" x 64",
by Lynn Spurlock,
Novato, CA, 2004

Dog Stars (right) is set with the classic Streak of Lightning arrangement, and *Bali Stars* (below) is a complex version of that old favorite.

Dog Stars, 54" x 75",
by the author, 2004

Bali Stars, 56" x 48",
by the author, 2001

Moving away from the classic multiple-star setting and using a single large star in the center of a multi-block quilt is Janyce Anderson's beautiful appliqué quilt *Rising Sun.* A single complex star like the 64-point design acts as a focal point in the quilt.

Rising Sun, 68" x 68",
by Janyce Anderson,
Carmel Valley, CA, 2001

Flashy stars are forever popular in the center of medallions. *Blooming Compass* features a large Twilight Star with elaborate borders. *Compass Rose Path* (page 18) is also a medallion, but with circular as well as classic Flying Geese, and the center stars are set on point within the quilt. *Malachite Star* (page 18) uses repetition of the geese motif to border the star with circling geese.

Blooming Compass, 56" x 57",
by Betty Whitman,
Aptos, CA, 2002

Malachite Star, 41" x 41",
by the author, 2001.
Hand-marbled fabric by
Marjorie Bevis.

Compass Rose Path,
94" x 94",
by Jetty Morton,
Suquamish, WA, 2002

Moonlight Medallion (right) is another quilt with a single-star center, set square but with stars on point in the outer border. This quilt was started as a round-robin. I contributed the center star, but as the "robin" progressed, only two other quilters— Ellen Cooper and Mary Flynn— contributed, so I stepped back in and added the rest of the stars and the remaining borders.

Points West (below), featuring a large star set on point with a pieced border and smaller stars in the corners, is a beautiful arrangement by Jeanne Thomas.

Moonlight Medallion, 57" x 57", by the author, with Ellen Cooper, Santa Rosa, CA, and Mary Flynn, Sebastopol, CA, 1998

Points West, 66" x 66", by Jeanne Thomas, Lake Oswego, OR, 2003. Quilted by Janet Fogg, Lake Oswego, OR.

Jan Krentz, a talented quilter and author, has designed two wonderful medallion quilts. *Sailor's Delight* (left), a tribute to her husband's naval career, commemorates sailing ships from different eras. *Underwear Islands* (below) celebrates the wonderful humorous fabrics now available to quilters.

Sailor's Delight, 48" x 48", by Jan Krentz, Poway, CA, 1992. Photo by Carina Woolrich, Woolrich Studios.

Underwear Islands, 44" x 44", by Jan Krentz, Poway, CA, 1993. Photo by Carina Woolrich, Woolrich Studios.

In *Carnival Star* (right), Susan Cleveland has created an amazing star medallion that features intricate piecing and elaborate appliqué.

A Few Compasses Between Friends (below) has everything: big flashy stars and pieced sashings and borders, as well as appliqué intersections and swags. A museum-quality antique quilt offered for sale on eBay inspired this quilt. Susan Rossi designed it and then completed it with help from her talented friend Gerry Sweem. It is interesting that there is another, almost identical antique quilt in the collection of the American Museum in Bath, England. I have admired that quilt for many years, as it is on the cover of the museum catalog. Some of the fabrics are even identical. What a mystery! Are the two older quilts by the same maker, relatives, or just two quilters from the same community?

Carnival Star, 64" x 82",
by Susan Cleveland,
Concord, MN, 2003

A Few Compasses Between Friends, 91" x 91", by Susan Rossi, Malibu, CA, and Gerry Sweem, Reseda, CA, 2003. Photo by Melissa Karlin Mahoney, courtesy of *Quilter's Newsletter Magazine*.

I created the quilt *New Directions* (right) after my book *Mariner's Compass Quilts: New Directions* was published in l995. I composed the background arrangement of chambray fabrics and then designed the stars to fit, using patterns and ideas from the book.

As I said at the beginning of this chapter, I see designs with circles as being the genesis for new star quilts. A trip to Paris and a stay in an old hotel provided the inspiration for *French Starflowers* (below). Leaded glass windows from the Art Deco period of the 1930s were featured in the hotel lobby. I was inspired by the original flowers, stems, leaves, and sky shapes to include my favorite stars and add lots of color. Notice that the stars were appliquéd to the background after an edge of bias tape had been applied outside the star circle. This served to separate the "starflowers" from one another and is reminiscent of the designs seen on old navigational charts.

Now let's move on to the technical aspects of creating Mariner's Compass and other star quilts.

New Directions, 76" x 92", by the author, 1996. In the collection of the Museum of the American Quilter's Society, Paducah, KY. Photo by Jack Mathieson.

French Starflowers,
75" x 89",
by the author, 2003

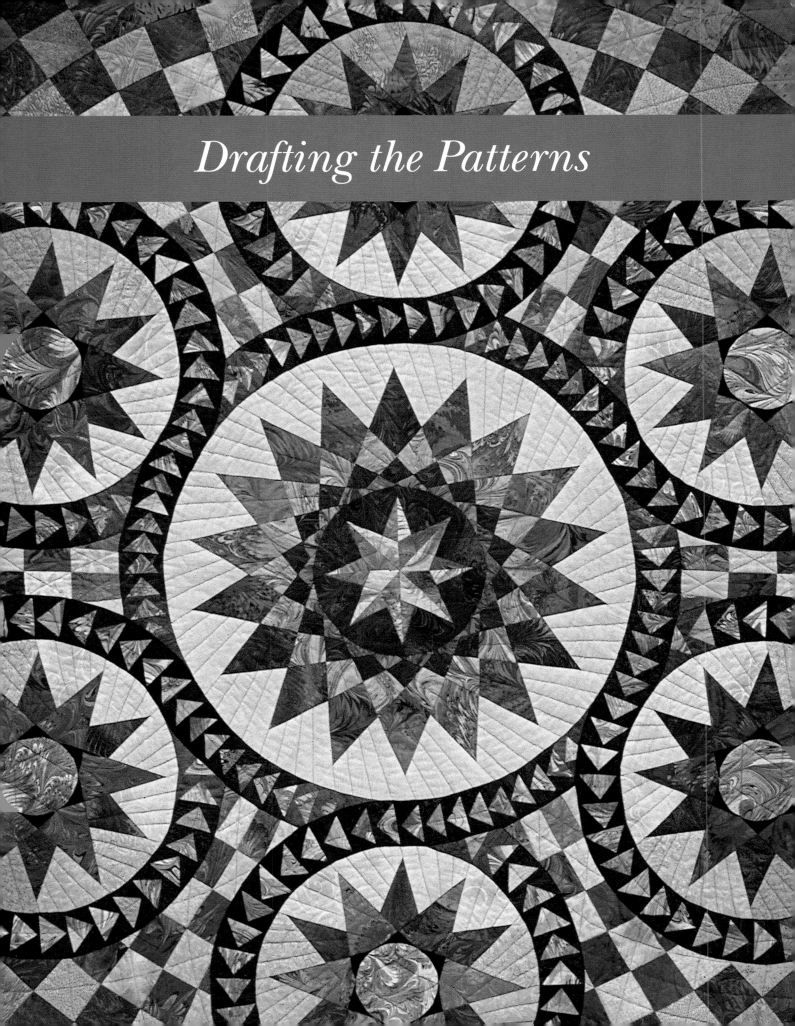

Daisy Star, 35" x 35", by the author, 2003

This book includes full-size patterns that I hope you will find useful. However, it isn't hard to draw radiating star designs using a compass and a ruler. The traditional symmetrical stars that use a set of repeating patterns must be drawn carefully and with as much accuracy as possible, especially if you plan to make templates. Full-size drawings on freezer paper give more flexibility and freedom, and accuracy is not as critical. If the pieces fit their neighbors when you draw and cut them apart, then they will fit when you sew them back together.

Supplies and Tools

Sharp Pencils and Eraser

Mechanical pencils with black lead in sizes 0.5mm or 0.7mm are excellent. You will find colored pencils (blue, red, and green) useful for the first exercise to help you identify the set of lines you are working with in each step.

Adjustable Drafting Compass

Compasses come in a variety of types and styles. If you are going to use one often, invest in one that stays fixed where you set it. Some styles have a handy quick-release mechanism, and some have an extension that allows them to make larger circles.

Freezer Paper

This plastic-coated paper is available in a variety of sizes from the following sources:
- Grocery stores typically carry freezer paper in rolls of various widths. If you can't find it on the grocery shelves, a full-service butcher might be willing to provide you with a small quantity.
- Quilt supply sources offer sheets printed with a ¼" grid.

- Office supply sources often sell freezer paper packaged in 8½" x 11" sheets for use with a computer printer.

Protractor

Available at art or drafting supply stores, this instrument helps lay down and measure angles. Use either the 180° (half circle) or 360° (full circle) size. The larger the protractor, the more accurate the angles you will be able to draw with it.

Clear Plastic Ruler With Holes

For large circles, you can use a yardstick compass, available from an art supply store or through various quilt supply sources. Some 18" plastic rulers come with drilled holes and can be used with a sharp pencil as a compass. As an alternative, you can drill holes in a ruler yourself to use for making large circles.

Graph Paper (¼" or ⅛" grid)

Use the 8½" x 11" size for the 6" practice exercises; 17" x 22" is available for larger designs. (Actually, plain paper is fine. I just like the grid marks to begin the squares and to use for reference as I go along.)

Drafting supplies and tools for drafting Mariner's Compass designs

Drafting Exercises

Circular Stars

Once you know how to draft a basic star, you can go on to make any size or variation. For this exercise, use a 6" square practice size. Work with the graph paper on a pad of paper (so that the drafting compass point doesn't move) and keep your pencils sharp. Hold the compass by the top, not the side arm. If you have trouble swinging the compass accurately, try holding it still and turning the paper under it.

EXERCISE 1: *The Circular Star*

Use a **black pencil** to draft points 1–4.

1. Draw a 6" square in the center of the graph paper and mark to divide it in half vertically, horizontally, and diagonally from corner to corner.

2. Set the compass point in the center and the pencil/marker arm ¼" in from the top of the square. (The background is easier to piece if the star is allowed to float inside the block.) Swing the compass to make this outer circle.

3. Draw a circle with a 1½" diameter in the center of the square (it will have a ¾" radius). This is the drafting circle and will determine the width of the rays. A good rule of thumb is to start with a circle approximately one-quarter the diameter of the outer circle. A small circle will make thin rays; a larger circle will make fat rays.

4. Use a ruler to draw slanted lines from the outside circle at A to the inside circle at B to create the sides of the four rays in the horizontal and vertical positions.

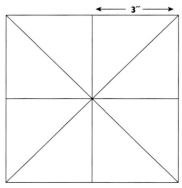

Step 1

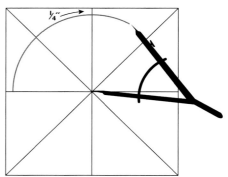

Step 2

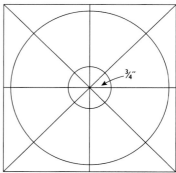

Step 3

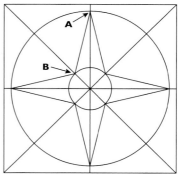

Step 4

Use a **red pencil** to draft points 5–8.

5. Draw slanted lines from the outside circle at C to the inside circle at D to create the sides of the four rays in the diagonal positions.

Use a **blue pencil** to draft points 9–16 with the bisecting technique.

6. Find the midpoint between two of the eight rays by bisecting the distance between E and F. Set the compass to the distance between E and F, and swing the compass from E into the area beyond the square and mark an arc. Move the compass so the point swings from F, and mark an arc that crosses the previous arc.

7. Place the ruler along the line from the center point and the crossing of the arcs and mark a dashed line showing the new 16th-point position on the outer circle and the inner circle. This technique is called bisecting and can be used to accurately divide any curved space in half.

8. Repeat Steps 6 and 7 around the entire circle.

9. Use the ruler to draw new rays by placing the ruler on the blue mark G on the outer circle and on the blue mark H on the inner circle. Intersection H is offset from the ray by 45° and can be found by counting over two radiating lines on the inside circle in this first bisection. Mark a solid line from G to the edge of the adjoining ray (the first intersecting line).

10. Repeat Step 9 around the circle to finish the 16 points.

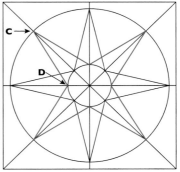

Step 5

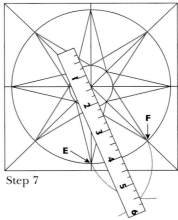

Step 6

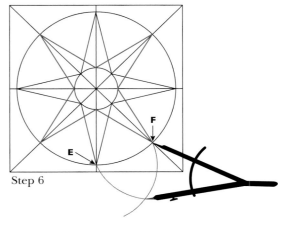

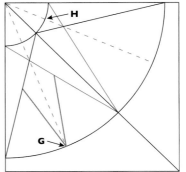

Step 7

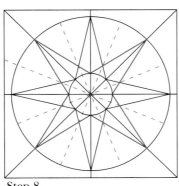

Step 8

Step 9

Use a **green pencil** to draft points 17–32.

11. To divide the star into 32 points, bisect it again using the new distance between the E and G rays. Count over four radiating lines on the inner circle to find the angle for the new ray in the next (32-point) bisection.

Traditional Mariner's Compass designs on quilts commonly have 16 to 32 points, although I have seen wonderful quilts with 64 points. A 16-point star has a spiky character, and the addition of 16 more points (32) not only doubles the number of pieces in the design but also tends to soften the star, giving it a rounder character. You can double the number of any division (e.g., 5 to 10, 6 to 12) by using the bisecting technique.

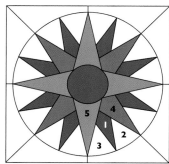

Step 11   E   G   4th line

Variations

At this stage of drafting, you have all the lines necessary to create the pattern shapes for making a 16- or 32-point star. It is not necessary to draft the complete design in order to have the pattern shapes for templates. However, it is helpful to have a complete design to help visualize both the fabric placement and the piecing sequence. I have given names to the basic stars. The numbers identify the pattern pieces necessary to construct these basic stars.

Another popular variation has the rays divided horizontally at the base. Use the compass to create a curved line or a ruler for a straight line.

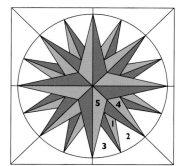

Split Star

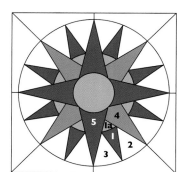

Sunburst with 16 points

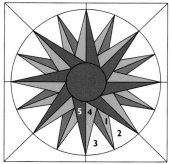

16-Point Swirling Star

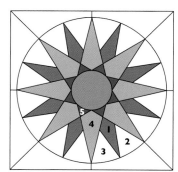

Starflower

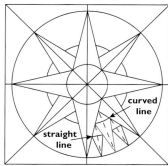

Rays divided horizontally

Concentric Circle Star

Variations are created by mixing rays of different widths or lengths.

A new outer ring can be drawn, and the ends of some rays will touch this new, smaller circle.

Internally Divided Stars

The previous stars were all drafted with different sizes of rays touching the outside drafting circle. Some of my favorite stars are those that have internal divisions that leave the outermost rays all the same length and width but create more spaces inside the stars that can be used for design purposes.

The illustration (top right) shows the basic Starflower design. The new designs are created during the drafting process by allowing the sides of the smallest pieces to overlay the previous stars. This creates the star in the style that I call Twilight Star (below right).

If you divide those spaces in half again with a vertical line, you create the star in the style I call Cartwheel Costa Rica.

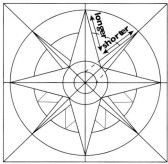

Rays of different widths and lengths

Basic Starflower with further divisions

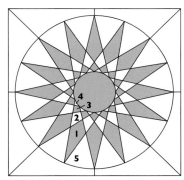

Twilight Star

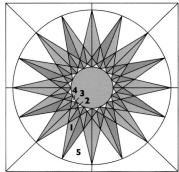

Cartwheel Costa Rica style

Annie's Quilt,
40" x 40",
by Linda Humphrey
and Jan Kolarov,
Los Osos, CA, 2004

**Amish Mariner's
Compass,** 58" x 58",
by Carroll Griffiths,
Modesto, CA, 2001

A further variation is possible based on the number of divisions in the star. The typical Mariner's Compass design is divided like a navigational compass so that it has a north, south, east, and west—4 points that can be divided into 8, 16, 32, or 64 points. Use a protractor to divide stars into other popular divisions based on 5, 6, or 9. It isn't necessary to draft the complete design in order to have the pattern shapes required for the foundations or templates. However, it is helpful to have a complete design to visualize the fabric placement and the piecing sequence.

EXERCISE 2: *Other Divisions*

Drafting a Star Divisible by Five

1. Draw a 6" square in the center of the graph paper and find the center. Draw a circle ¼" inside the square.

2. Align the center of the protractor (intersection of 90 and 0/180) with the center of the circle.

3. Use the protractor to mark every 72° (72, 144, 216, 288, 0/360). To mark points beyond 180°, reverse the protractor and use 180 less. For example, for 216° use 36° (216 − 180 = 36).

4. Once you have divided the circle into five sections, draw a drafting circle (page 26) and use the ruler to draw the sides of the rays. Use the bisecting technique presented on page 27 to further divide the spaces.

Drafting a Star Divisible by Six

Use the instructions for Drafting a Star Divisible by Five, but this time mark every 60° (60, 120, 180, 240, 300, 0/360).

Drafting a Star Divisible by Nine

Use the instructions for Drafting a Star Divisible by Five, but this time mark every 40° (40, 80, 120, 160, 200, 240, 280, 320, 0/360).

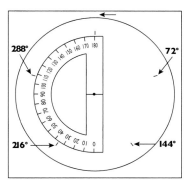

Steps 1, 2, and 3

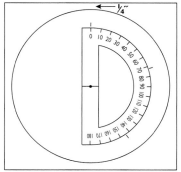

Step 3 continued

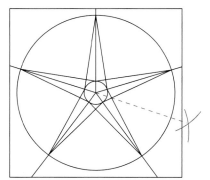

Step 4

Outside Shapes

Circles are the traditional shape for radiating stars, probably because it is not difficult to piece the gently curving shape into background fabric. However, it is certainly possible to draw the star into almost any shape, as shown below. When drafting the rays, draw the points to the edge of your outside shape or allow them to float within, just as you would for drafting a star in a circle.

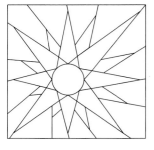 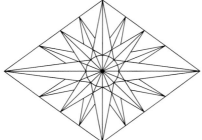

The oval is a graceful classic shape that quilt-makers admire. It is easy to piece into a background even though the piecing is more complex, as the star has more pattern shapes, and it may be necessary to reverse the pattern pieces.

An oval is longer than it is wide. My advice is to first explore where you want to put this oval. You may already have the shape you need in an oval hoop, tabletop, silver tray, or the dimensions of a double bed. Use that shape to determine the proportion of your oval (length and width). However, if you are starting from scratch, a good rule of thumb is to make the oval one-half longer than it is wide—for example, 20" x 30".

The most graceful oval maintains the relationship between the length and the width around the curve. There are a number of ways to draft the "perfect" oval. The paper-tape method is my favorite.

The Stars Are Smiling at You, 82" x 64", by Judy Jordan-Biesele, Santa Clara, CA, 2004

EXERCISE 3: *The Oval Star Using the*
Paper-Tape Method

1. Cut a strip of paper ½" wide from the bottom of the graph paper to use later as your drafting tool.

2. Draw a 4" square and make it into a rectangle by adding 1" at the top and 1" at the bottom.

3. Mark diagonal lines through the corners of the square and horizontal/vertical lines through the center of the rectangle.

4. Mark positions ¼" inside the rectangle to establish where the oval will float inside the rectangle. Name these positions A and B with Ø as the center.

5. On the strip of paper tape, mark ½" from the end as the lowercase letter ø; then mark the distance from Ø to B (name it with a lowercase b) and Ø to A (name it with a lowercase a).

6. Use the paper tape to make a series of dots that can be connected to create the oval. Begin by placing the paper tape on the horizontal line so that ø is at B and b is at Ø. Now move the tape down line A while keeping the b on line A and the a on line B, and mark points at ø. Continue moving the tape and making marks at ø.

7. Mark the complete oval, or fold and trace to repeat the second half.

8. To draft a star inside the oval, choose either a circle or oval for the center. For an oval center, refer to Steps 4–7 (above). Use a protractor to mark additional divisions.

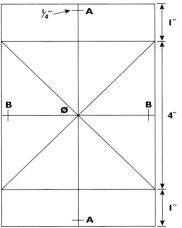

Steps 2, 3, and 4

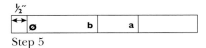

Step 5

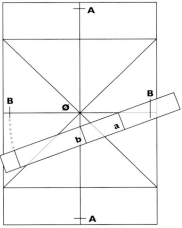

Step 6

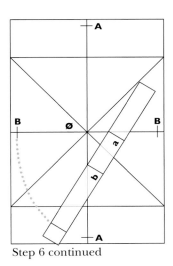

Step 6 continued

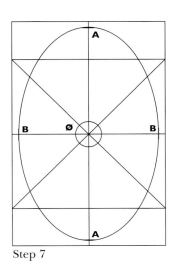

Step 7

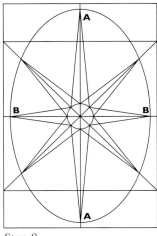

Step 8

Another way to mark additional divisions is to use a ruler, as shown at left.

Place the ruler on the intersections C and D, and draw a line through these two intersections.

Templates for a symmetrical star in an oval can be made in the traditional way, but I have found that foundations, drafted full size, work well because of the number of different-sized pieces and possible reversals. Patterns for two oval compass designs appear on the pullout at the back of the book.

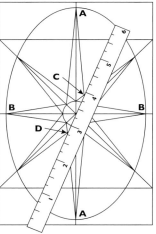

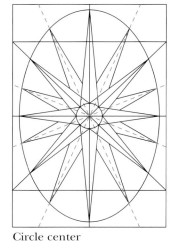
Circle center

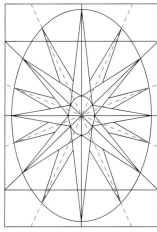
Oval center

Black Hole Quencher,
61" x 61", by Joyce Balzley,
Bremerton, WA, 2000.
Quilted by Lori Kelley,
Petaluma, CA.

Encompassed, 41" x 41", by Lyric Kinard,
Cary, NC, with Barbara Molnar, Jan Beasley,
Karen Zeher, Mary Stone, and Amy Winsor, 1998

EXERCISE 4: *Off-Center Star*

The radiating lines in the star can be placed off center in any shape desired.

1. Draw a 6" square and mark the center point and one diagonal. Set the compass pointer in the center with the pencil/marker arm ¼" in from the square. Swing the compass to make the outer circle.

2. Set the compass to ¾" and set the pencil/marker arm in the center with the pointer arm up the diagonal line to the right. Swing from the compass pointer so that the drafting circle is off-center.

3. Draw horizontal and vertical lines through the new center, using the edge of the square block to position your ruler. The remaining diagonal line is drawn at a right angle (90°) to the first diagonal. Use a vertical line on your ruler as a reference to line up the first diagonal.

4. Continue with the circular star drafting as in Step 4 on page 26.

5. Use a ruler to divide for new ray positions.

You can apply all the variations discussed so far to this star. Since there are so many pattern pieces in the off-center variations, foundation techniques work well. Just remember to number the pieces to match your original design if you trace onto template material or freezer paper. Make a "map" if you draft directly onto the freezer paper. If you draft onto the dull side of the freezer paper, your design will be reversed when it is assembled and sewn. If you find this confusing, draw the design on the shiny side of the freezer paper with a fine-point permanent pen. Label the pieces on both the shiny and dull sides.

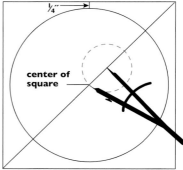

Steps 1 and 2

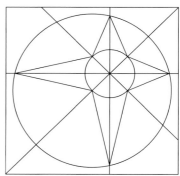

Steps 3 and 4

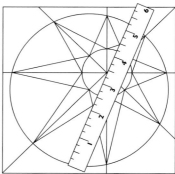

Step 5

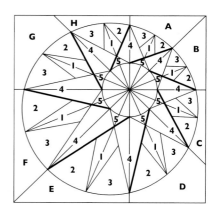

Kitchen Compass III, 66" x 30", by Iris Frank, Santa Cruz, CA, 2004

Designs Outside the Stars

Now that we have drafted a variety of stars within the circle, we can think about how to add interesting designs *outside* the star circle.

Circling geese, outer rings of points, and expanding checkerboard backgrounds are all extensions of the basic radiating lines and concentric circles.

The star shown below is the basic Starflower (page 28) with a new circle drawn around the outside of the star. Extend the drafting lines from the star points into that new circle to establish a set of wedges. You can divide those wedges into smaller units as desired. The circling geese pattern in Ann Shuken's *Directional Interpretation* (below right) has 32 units.

Star of St. Mark's, 21" x 21", by the author, 2000

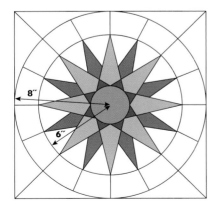

Directional Interpretation, 30" x 30", by Ann Shuken, Fresno, CA, 2004. Quilted by Tanya Kochergen, Fresno, CA.

For the circling geese, draw another circle within the ring of wedges to establish the center line for the tips of the triangles, and then use a ruler to draw the sides of the triangles as shown. This illustration also shows an alternate choice: the outer ring of points. For an example, see *Hawaii Star* (page 68).

You can add more new design elements by adding more concentric circles around the stars. You can also increase the numbers of outer rings of points or add more circling geese. An example of the latter can be found in *Nautical Stars* (page 46), a quilt I made in 1986. This quilt has five rows of geese around a large star. As I look at this quilt today, my first thought is always, "How I wish I had known about paper-foundation techniques!"

Expanding Checkerboard

This design is created by extending the radiating lines farther and then drawing more concentric circles.

You can draft this pattern by using only one-eighth of the design and then using the pattern to create four foundations and four reversals. On my patterns, I converted the curved lines created in the concentric circles to straight lines because they are easier to sew. You can avoid using a compass to create the circles, and instead just mark the expanding lines with the desired distance and then connect those marks with a ruler. See Pattern 5 on the pullout.

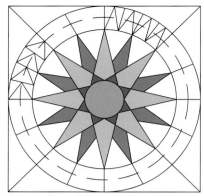

Outer ring of geese or points

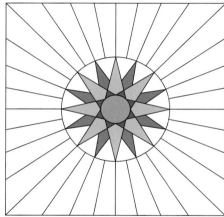

Extend radiating lines.

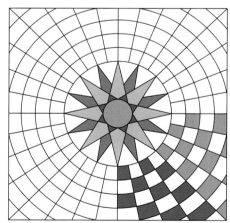

The lighter value shows the reversed checkerboard pattern.

Mariner's Surround, 41" x 41",
by Jan Fitzhugh, Twin Falls, ID, 2004.
Quilted by Ann Trotter, Filer, ID.

The diagrams at right illustrate the expanding checkerboard used with a simple star, circling geese, and outer ring of points.

After you have practiced the basic drafting exercises, you are ready to design your full-size star. Clear your table or drafting surface and assemble your tools, sharp pencils, and full-size paper. Choose from all the design variations presented and begin to create your own original star.

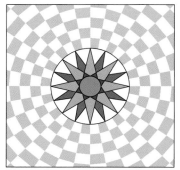

Expanding checkerboard with simple star

Expanding checkerboard with circling geese

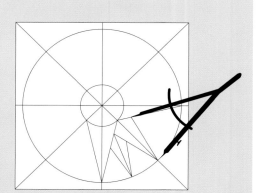

Expanding checkerboard with outer ring of points

Checklist of Possible Variations

When drafting stars that radiate from a center:

1. Size: How big do you want your star to be?

2. Outside Shape: Will it be round, oval, square, hexagonal, triangular, or some other shape?

3. Inside Drafting Shape: Will it be round or oval?

4. Position of Inside Drafting Shape: Will it be in the center, off-center up, off-center right, or some other variation?

5. Number of Basic Divisions: Will it be four, five, six, eight, or nine?

6. Width of the Rays: Will they be wide or narrow? This is determined by the size of the inside drafting shape.

7. Length of the Rays: This is determined by the outside shape or internal sets of concentric circles.

8. Divisions Within the Rays: Are they vertical (split), horizontal (concentric circle), diagonal (Starflower, Twilight Star, Cartwheel)?

If you are drafting a partial design in order to make templates or foundations, you can use the drafting compass or dividers to check the length of both sides of each ray or piecing wedge to be sure they all fit together accurately. Dividers look like a compass but have two sharp points (no pencil). They are more accurate than a traditional compass.

If you are drafting or tracing one-time-only patterns onto freezer paper, be sure that they are numbered to match your original design or a "map" that reminds you how the pieces fit together.

Marbled Stars, 47" x 52", by the author, 2000

Selecting Fabric

Sea and Stars, 27" x 27",
by Marianne Watada,
Santa Rosa, CA, 2004

Most quilters agree that it is the fabric that draws us to this craft, and the personal way we use it is what keeps us excited about the quilts we make.

I prefer 100% cotton fabric because it is the easiest to use. I recommend that you select fabrics that are similar to each other, and avoid fabrics that are loosely woven. Quilters have differing opinions on whether fabrics should be prewashed or used right from the bolt. Either way, be sure to test for bleeding, as the fabric may encounter water or steam at some time during the construction process.

Test for bleeding by wetting a small sample of the fabric. Put the dampened fabric on a white paper towel or white cloth and allow the fabric to dry. If there is significant color transfer, wash the fabric. If it still bleeds after a second washing, select another fabric.

The hardest part of making a quilt (as well as the most exciting) is selecting the fabric. I often hear quilters say that choosing color is the hardest part. For me, the fabric choice includes the variables of color and value as well as texture, scale, and style for print fabrics. I tend to let my emotions guide me in my color choices. Most quilters won't work with colors they don't like, and you can usually trust yourself in this area. However, this is not to say that studying color won't improve your work and give you confidence.

Contrast in value (the degree of lightness and darkness) is the element that seems most important to me in the Mariner's Compass design. Much of the charm of these stars comes from the crisp, delicate nature of the long rays, and contrast in value is what makes them work.

If you want your stars to show prominently, start by selecting the background fabric, and then choose fabrics that will show up on it after they have been reduced to sharply pointed rays.

To experiment with your choices, fold the fabrics twice and then overlap them onto the background fabric in the same order and general arrangement in which they will appear after they are sewn. This will give you a chance to see if the value differences hold up when the fabrics are reduced to sharply pointed rays.

First fold

Second fold

Audition fabrics.

The fabric in the pie-shaped background pieces will normally change grainline as the pieces move around the circle. If the fabric is directional, you will probably want to choose a different or compatible fabric for the background square. Select a fabric that has a nondirectional print if you want the circle of the star to blend in with the block background.

Quiltmakers often choose light-value backgrounds because these fabrics allow the broadest choice of color, but I favor dark backgrounds because they make the stars sparkle!

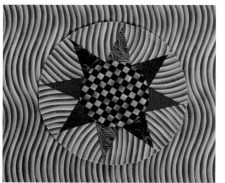

Grainline changes around the circle.

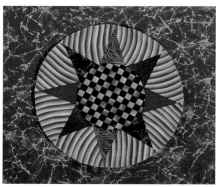

Compatible background square fabric

Backgrounds blend.

Starlight, Starbright,
53" x 51",
by Janyce Anderson,
Carmel Valley, CA, 2001

It is certainly possible to use a range of different fabrics in similar values for the star backgrounds, as I did in *Walking the Dog*.

Detail of ***Walking the Dog***

Walking the Dog,
48" x 48",
by the author, 2002

Another approach is to use changing values in the background, as I did in *Nautical Stars.* This can be quite a challenge, as you must change the values of the fabrics used in the rays as the values change in the background, but the results are certainly worth it.

Nautical Stars, 73" x 88", by the author, 1986. Photo by Jack Mathieson.

The fabrics used in the rays can be more varied than the background, but there is not a lot of area in the skinny rays. Use fabrics with larger-scale prints in the larger rays. If a fabric has areas where the print is the same value as the background, take care that the areas of similar value do not fall at the tip of a ray. This can cause the tip to blend with the background, making the tip appear blunted.

Directional fabrics such as stripes and plaids can add a lot of energy to these star designs. You can either control the placement of these fabrics by following the angles of the ray or ignore it, as the mood strikes you.

If you have selected a star design with a circle in the center, avoid using fabrics of the same value as the background, or the circle will tend to "drop out" and create a visual hole in the design.

On the other hand, fabrics with the same value as the background are good choices for designs that have a star in the center; the center star will appear to float over the background.

Designs with horizontal divisions in the rays are effective when they incorporate background-value fabrics, as these fabrics allow you to "look through" the star into the background. The main star in *Mariner's Lighthouse* (below) has a light, lacy appearance.

Tip of ray appears blunted.

Directional fabric options

Detail of **New Directions** (page 22). Background creates a visual hole.

Mariner's Lighthouse, 46" x 34", by Gloria Kennedy, Northridge, CA, 2001

Detail of **New Directions** (page 22). Star appears to float.

Circling geese offer two possibilities. If you use background fabric in the "path" behind the geese, the geese appear to circle in the same plane as the star. For an example, see *Directional Interpretation* (page 37). If you create a path that contrasts in value, the path confines the star and assumes more importance in the overall design. See *Malachite Star* (page 18) for an example. Outer rings of points are probably most successful if they continue the star plan. Use the same fabrics as the star in the same background as the star.

I've given my reasons for choosing fabrics in certain situations, but—of course—there is always a good reason for doing just the opposite. My *French Starflowers* quilts (right and on page 22) are good examples. In these quilts, I reduced the contrast in the star and background values so the stars would look more like flowers with multicolored petals.

In summary, my advice for fabric selection is to first decide the relative value of the fabrics you plan to use. Can you clearly detect the difference between the fabrics that will be placed beside each other? The contrast in value is what ultimately allows you to see the design.

TIP If you aren't happy with the color, try sparking it up by introducing a bit of the complementary color—the opposite color on the color wheel. Think of this as adding a little of the opposite amount of "temperature." In a warm-colored quilt (red, orange, yellow), add some cool (blue, green, violet), and vice versa.

French Starflowers Petite, 24" x 62", by the author, 2003

Construction

Dolphin Star, 29" x 29", by the author, 2003

No matter how inspiring your design and how wonderfully effective your fabric choices, you probably won't be happy with the results if your construction skills don't meet the challenge. The beauty of this design lies in those sharp and sometimes skinny rays, so the most important aspect of Mariner's Compass construction is accuracy.

Traditional methods of making templates and marking fabric work very well if you sew accurately through the intersections and don't allow the many bias edges to stretch. I still find this the best method for hand piecing.

Sewing onto paper foundations by sewing directly through the paper pattern produces very accurate results and is especially successful when you are working with very small piecing units, such as those you might encounter in miniatures. The paper stabilizes the bias edges and prevents them from stretching during the sewing process.

For several years, I have been working with a method that uses freezer paper but does not require sewing through the paper. Since I don't sew through the paper, I don't need to tear the paper out when I am finished sewing. Instead, I pull the freezer-paper foundations off the fabric at the completion of the sewing process. This usually allows me to reuse the foundations several times. It also allows me flexibility in the direction I press the seam allowances.

The patterns in this book are presented as foundations. If you wish to use traditional methods of hand or machine sewing with templates, you can trace the pattern shapes and assemble them using your chosen method.

Foundation Piecing

As I have mentioned, I prefer to use freezer-paper foundations that do not require sewing through the paper. If you prefer to use the traditional paper-foundation method, you'll find it covered briefly on page 55.

Preparing Foundations

You will need to prepare a copy of each segment of the pattern. For example, if the pattern has eight segments, you will need to make a copy of each. (If you photocopy the pattern, check to make sure that all the copies are accurate.) When I prepare foundations for the perforated freezer-paper method, I layer the pattern over a stack of freezer-paper sheets and then use an unthreaded needle on my sewing machine to stitch through the pattern and the layered paper.

Fabric Preparation

Foundation-piecing methods require that fabric pieces be cut oversized, so they have "placement" room—not just the standard ¼" seam allowance to which the piece will ultimately be trimmed. Fabrics can be precut into squares, rectangles, or "chunks" that you are sure are sufficiently large to cover the area of the pattern shape. I usually prepare a precutting template to ensure that I will have adequate fabric to cover the shape (see page 52).

By precutting the fabrics into approximately the correct shape, I can select grainlines and even preselect print designs. Since the fabrics are cut only to approximate size, it is sometimes possible to stack them and cut several pieces at once. Also, since the template is made from freezer paper, I can iron it (shiny side down) to the fabric and then remove and reuse the template (see Steps 4 and 5, page 52).

Sewing

I usually use thread in neutral colors such as black, white, and shades of gray for piecing. Since the seams of the rays cross over each other, I generally select a thread in a value similar to the fabric of the rays, not the background fabric.

When using the perforated freezer-paper method, choose a stitch length similar to the one you use for sewing regular seams. *Do not use the tiny stitches typical for traditional foundation piecing.* I usually set my machine to sew 12 to 15 stitches to the inch (2.5 on imported machines).

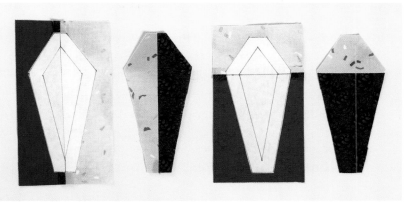

Presewn ray fabrics

The rays in some of the star designs are split so that a dark value and a light value run vertically or horizontally through the rays. In some cases, these contrasting fabrics can be presewn.

If you are careful not to sew through the freezer paper, you can save and reuse it. While it is possible when the segments are attached to each other to stitch the seams with the freezer paper on both sides, I find that I am more successful if I roll back the paper foundation on the wrong side before I stitch (see Step 15, page 54). You can remove the paper if you stitch through it accidentally, but since you are using a regular-sized stitch, the seam tends to distort as the paper is removed.

Perforated Freezer-Paper Foundations

The following steps walk you through the process of piecing the basic 16-point Starflower variation using the perforated freezer-paper foundation method. Other patterns involve slightly different piecing sequences, but they are all closely related. If you have drafted your own pattern, find the pattern on pages 59–86 that most closely resembles the piecing sequence.

1. Trace or photocopy each unique segment of the design. Place the copy on a stack of four to five pieces of freezer paper, all with shiny sides up. Fasten the copy and the freezer paper together temporarily with staples, or use the *tip* of a hot, dry iron at the x's on the pattern to adhere the layers.

2. Set the stitch length on the sewing machine to 12 to 15 stitches to the inch (2.5 on imported machines). Use an unthreaded sewing machine needle to stitch on each of the sewing lines of the pattern. If you prepare many foundations, you may want to use an old or already dulled needle.

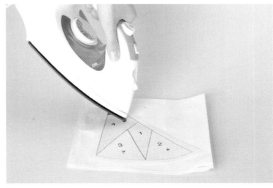

Step 1

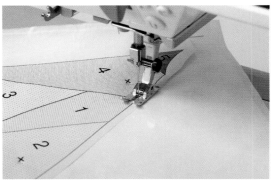

Step 2

3. Remove the pattern from the freezer paper and save for reuse at another time. Cut the marked freezer-paper foundations into the desired segments on the outside line. If you are careful, you may be able to cut the whole stack (four or five sheets) at once. Be sure to remove the paper from the edges of the seamline. Transfer any numbers or letters from the original pattern onto the dull side of the freezer paper foundation.

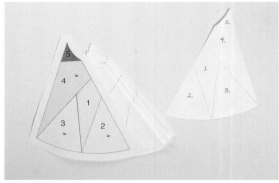
Step 3

4. Use the original pattern to trace a template for each unique shape onto freezer paper. Add ½" to each edge of the original pattern shape. Use this template to cut the fabrics. (If the piece is a triangle with a blunted point (e.g., piece 5 on the ray pattern on page 78), you can "complete" the triangle when you cut the fabric.) It isn't necessary to cut these fabrics precisely, as the ½" allows for the positioning necessary with foundation techniques. All the seam allowances on the fabric pieces will be trimmed to ¼" as the sewing progresses.

Step 4

 Unless you are using fabrics with a directional print, you can stack the fabrics before you press the template in place and cut multiple layers at one time.

5. Iron the entire freezer-paper foundation to a piece of muslin or scrap fabric, and then remove it, before you begin piecing. This removes the shine from the freezer paper and helps the presser foot glide more easily as you sew. Use a hot, dry iron to adhere the once-shiny side of the freezer paper to the wrong side of Fabric 1.

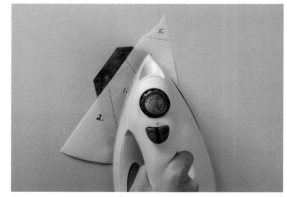
Step 5

6. Fold the freezer paper back on the perforations between Paper Areas 1 and 2 to expose the seamline. Place Fabric 2 right sides together with Fabric 1. Check to make sure that Paper Area 2 is completely covered by Fabric 2.

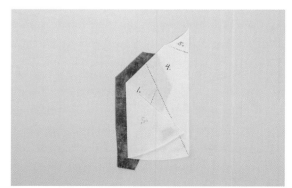
Step 6

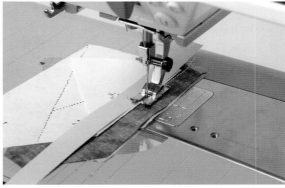

7. Stitch along the edge of the folded freezer paper through the two fabrics. If the presser foot hangs up on the sticky side of the freezer paper, place a strip of paper along the edge of the freezer paper to block the sticky side. A nonstick (Teflon) presser foot will help as well.

8. Trim the seam allowance to ¼", fold the paper back, and press the fabric to the freezer paper. If Fabric 1 is darker than Fabric 2, grade the seam so that the lighter fabric extends beyond the darker fabric.

Step 7

9. Fold back the paper on the perforations along Paper Area 3 and place Fabric 3 right sides together with Fabric 1. Make sure that Fabric 3 completely covers Paper Area 3. Stitch along the edge of the freezer paper through the fabric layers. Be sure that the line of stitching crosses over the previous line of stitching to form a sharp point at the edge of the freezer paper.

10. Trim and press. Fold back on the perforations and position Fabric 4. Stitch along the edge of the freezer paper through the fabric layers.

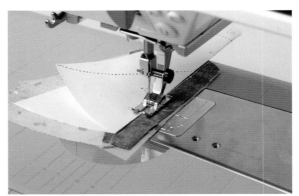

Step 8

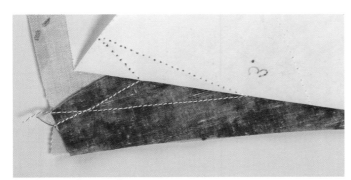

Stitching a sharp point

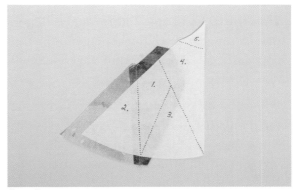

Step 9

Step 10

11. Trim and press the seam allowance away from Fabric 4, toward the background fabric (Fabrics 1/3). I like to press all the seam allowances toward the background fabric so my star points are crisp and free of seam allowances. I adjust the direction of the seams as I go along by temporarily pulling the freezer paper back from the seam about ½".

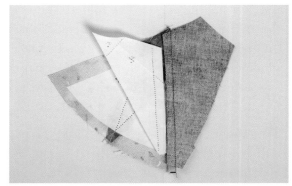

Step 11

12. Press Paper Area 4 back over Fabric 4. Fold back Paper Area 5.

13. Position Fabric 5 along the edge of Fabric 4. Stitch, trim, and press.

14. Press the freezer-paper foundation well to make sure that all the seams are fully open and the freezer paper is secure. Trim around the completed foundation, leaving a ¼" seam allowance.

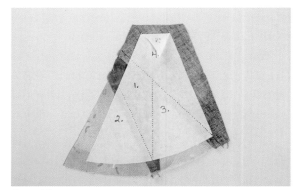

Step 12

15. When you have completed all the segments, pin them together at the intersections in sets of two along the side of Fabrics 4/5. Place the pins in the segment on the side along Paper Area 4/5 so you can ensure that your stitching creates a sharp point at the tip of the star.

To avoid sewing through the paper on the back of the segments, temporarily pull the freezer paper away (about ½") on the back side of the two-segment unit. Stitch on the front side with the pins, and then press the seam allowances under the paper, toward the background fabric.

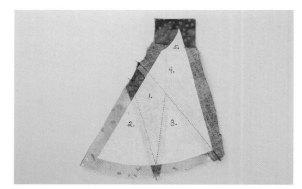

Step 13

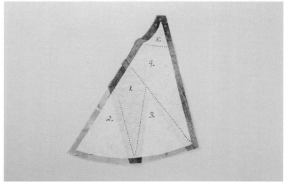

Step 14

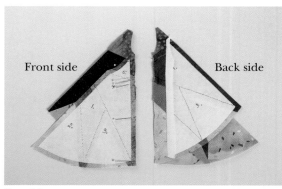

Front side   Back side

Step 15

16. Sew the pieced two-segment units into larger units until you have pieced the entire star. Press the star flat with the seam allowances toward the background fabric, away from the star points.

17. Remove the paper foundations by pulling them gently away from the fabrics. Check to make sure that you are not fraying the seams as you remove the paper, and pull the paper in a different direction if you encounter fraying. You can usually reuse the foundations after removing any loose threads.

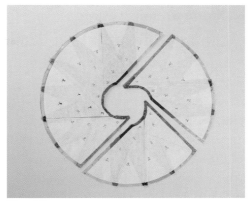

Step 16

Piecing for Split-Star Variations

When you are constructing a star with split rays, such as the Swirling Star (pages 62 and 71) or Cartwheel Costa Rica (page 80), orient the presewn ray fabric as shown. Note how the paper foundation 4/5 line aligns with the presewn ray seamline.

Traditional Paper Foundations:
Stitching Through the Paper

You can trace, photocopy, or scan paper foundations into a computer and then print the required quantity onto regular paper, vellum, or other crisp, thin specialty paper. You can even print foundations onto freezer paper if the paper is properly prepared or purchased for that use. The thinner and crisper the paper, the easier it will be to remove after sewing.

For traditional methods, you will use the same patterns as for the freezer-paper method, but you must leave a ¼"-wide seam allowance around the outside edge. You will stitch through the line on the paper rather than directly on the exposed fabric along the folded edge of the paper foundation.

Shorten your sewing machine stitch length to about 20 stitches per inch and use a larger needle (90/14) to help pierce the paper and allow for easy removal. Position the layers of fabric on the back side of the pattern and stitch through the fabric/paper layers on the front side of the paper using the marked lines as a guide.

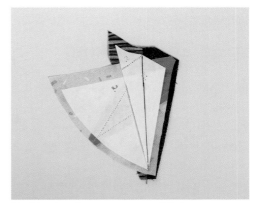

Positioning for presewn ray fabrics

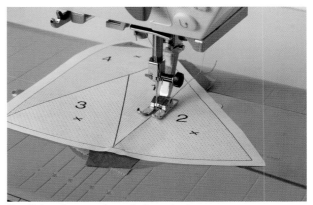

Traditional paper-foundation piecing

Finishing the Round Center

Prepare the center by tracing the pattern onto freezer paper. Iron the paper shiny side down to the wrong side of the fabric and cut out the shape, leaving a ¼" seam allowance. Remove the freezer paper and pin it shiny side up to the wrong side of the fabric. Use the tip of a hot iron to press the seam allowances to the template as shown.

Fold the circle into quarters to make match marks and pin it to the pieced star block. Appliqué the circle in place by hand or machine with matching-colored thread. Remove the freezer-paper circle.

You can also thread baste the center.

Pressing and Blocking

Hand-pieced blocks can be pressed after the sewing is completed. Paper foundations can be pressed as you go. Perforated freezer-paper foundations *must* be pressed with a dry, hot iron during the assembly. Be sure to press the seam allowances away from the tips of the rays if possible.

The major challenge with radiating star designs is their tendency to form volcano or funnel shapes after they are stitched, rather than nice flat circles. It is hard to cut so many pieces accurately from fabric (which tends to distort) and then to sew them back together so that you still have a 360° circle. It is especially hard using the sewing machine, which puts a certain amount of tension into the stitched seam. Foundation piecing solves many of these problems, but I always block the stars upon completion. In some cases, blocking helps to completely open the seams and encourage the star to flatten. This is especially true on the split-to-center designs (page 65).

You will need a flat surface to which you can pin and then press. An ironing board works well for small stars. If you don't have a large pin board, lay a towel on a firm carpeted surface. Pin the star to the flat surface, beginning with the tips of the vertical rays and then moving to the horizontal rays, easing them flat. Continue around the circle, pinning opposing points until the star is flat. Press with a steam iron. Do not remove the star from the pin board until the fabric is cool and dry. If the star is too small to press, pin it to the board, spray it with a fine mist of water, and allow it to dry.

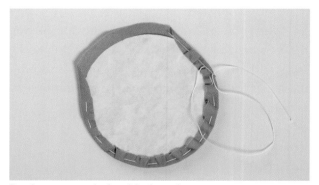

Basting center circle with an iron

Basting center circle with thread

Attaching Stars to the Background

If you have pieced the star into a circle, there are several basic ways to get it into a background. Patterns for the background blocks appear on the pullout at the back of the book.

Method 1: Insert the star circle into a pieced background block.

This is the most time- and fabric-efficient method. Prepare four quarter-circle background pieces and sew them together. Press the seams open. Be sure to mark the star point positions on the wrong side of the background fabric. Pin the star into the background, using the matching marks for the points of the rays of the star, and then sew. Press the seam allowances toward the background.

Method 2: Piece the star circle into a solid background.

Position the star circle on the wrong side of the desired background fabric. Mark around the outside of the star circle seam allowance (which has been trimmed to ¼"). Be sure to mark the star point positions on the background fabric. Remove the star circle and measure ½" inside the marked circle. Cut and remove the inner circle of fabric. Pin the star circle into the cut circle, matching the points. Sew by hand or machine and press the seam allowances to the background.

Method 3: Appliqué the star circle to the background.

This method allows you to position the star anywhere on a quilt surface. I generally prefer to appliqué with hand stitching, but machine methods of top stitching, blind stitching, or decorative stitching work well also.

Baste the star circle seam allowances under ¼" and pin in the desired position on the quilt top. Appliqué by hand or machine.

Remove the top basting and cut the background fabric away from behind the block, leaving a ¼" seam allowance. Clip this seam if necessary and press away from the star if desired.

Method 1

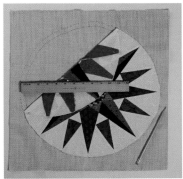

Method 2: Mark star-point positions on background fabric.

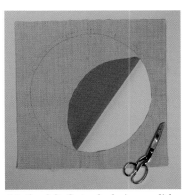

Method 2: Cut a hole in a solid background.

Method 3: Baste and pin.

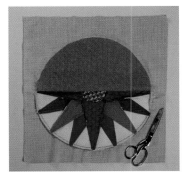

Method 3: Cut away the background.

Quilting

A goal in planning the quilting is to have relatively consistent amounts of quilting throughout the piece. An obvious quilting design is one that radiates in the same way as the star. (If the piecing creates a bit of a volcano, the quilting should help control it.) If you choose this kind of quilting design, make sure that all the lines of quilting do not come all the way into the center.

Overlaying the star design with another set of points is effective at filling the space.

The star designs lend themselves well to structural quilting, or quilting within the pieces themselves. If the seam allowances have been pressed away from the tips, it is easy to quilt inside the rays near or ½" in from the seam allowances. Large stars with more area in the rays may need extra fill quilting. Quilting lines extending from the points of the rays along one side of the seam create a spiral. You can add more divisions between the points to enhance the spiral effect.

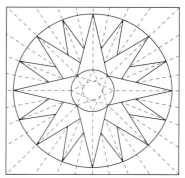

Radiating quilting lines

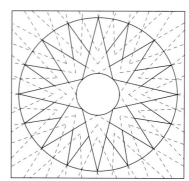

Overlay quilting lines

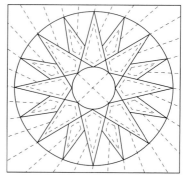

Structural quilting lines with spiral effect

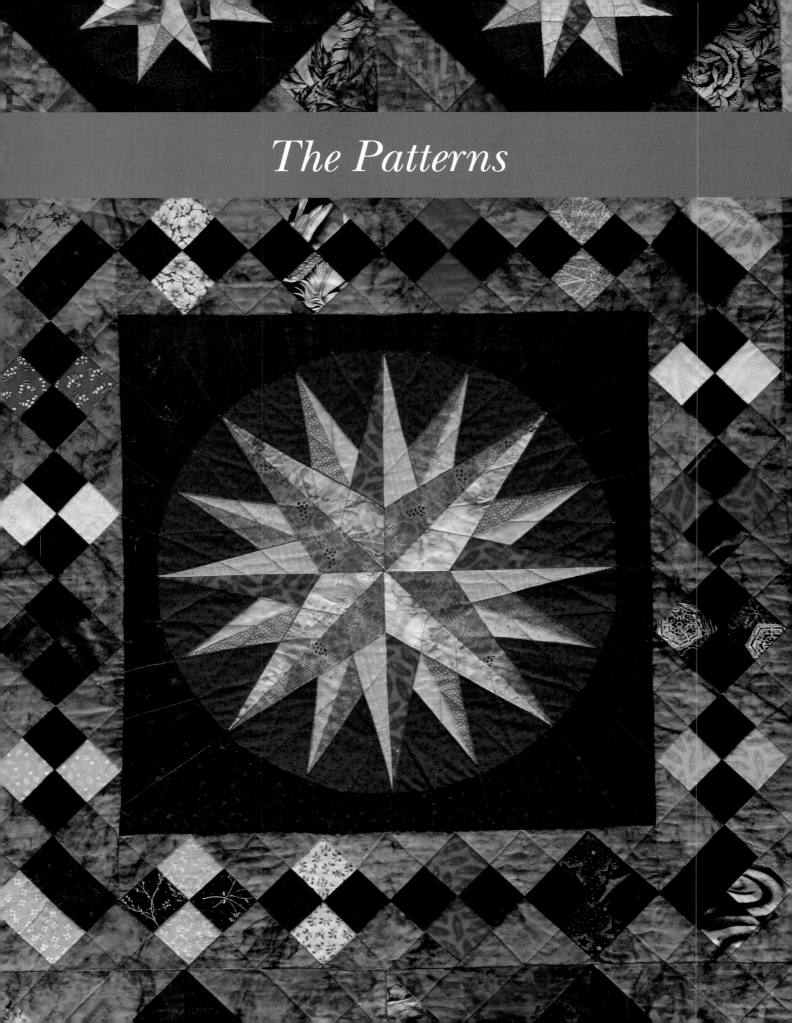

The Patterns

This is a good pattern to begin with if you have never sewn a radiating star. It has a minimum number of points and only a few pattern shapes. See page 50 for general instructions.

You can see examples of this pattern in *Dog Stars* (detail below) and *Bali Stars* (page 15). It is also the pattern for the center of the 64-point star in *Pulsar* (page 92).

FABRIC CUTTING PLAN

Refer to pages 50 and 52 to precut fabric into oversized shapes.

A: Cut 8 (star points).
B: Cut 8 (background).
Center circle: Cut 1.

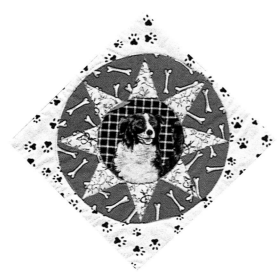

Detail of **Dog Stars.** See page 15 for a full view of this quilt.

Pattern I

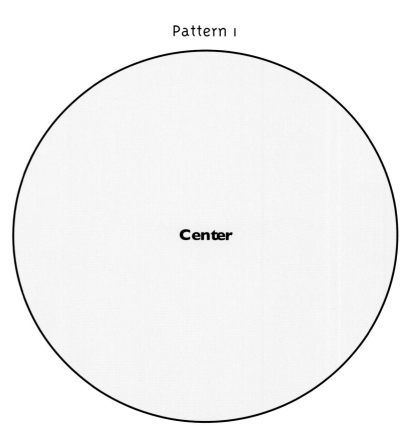

Center

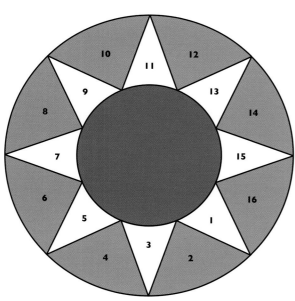

Piecing sequence

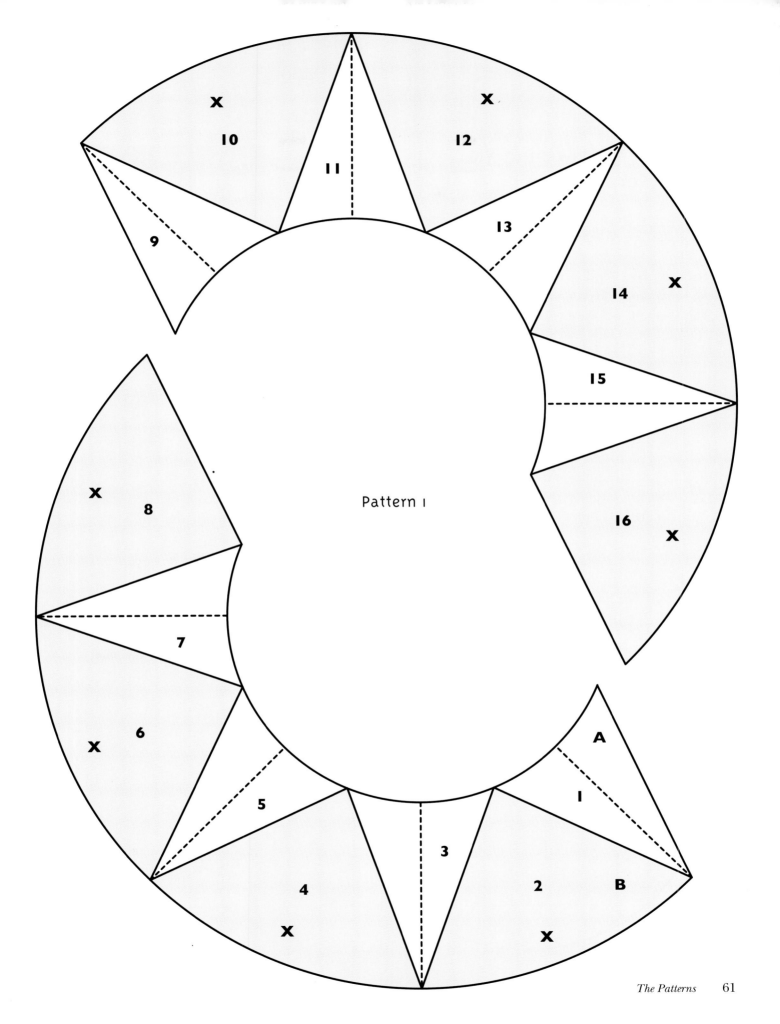

Pattern 1

Starflower and Swirling Star With 32-Point Option

This basic pattern can be arranged in a number of combinations. For examples, see *Fishy Star* (page 4), *Daisy Star* (page 24), *Star of Provence* (page 74), *Chocolate Swirl* (page 70), *Dolphin Star* (page 49), and *Yellow Marbled Star* (page 67). It is my favorite star because it goes together so quickly in its simplest form, and yet it has so many design possibilities.

The 16-point stars have 8 foundations. The 32-point stars have a 2-part foundation that is stitched back together before the basic 8 foundations are joined.

 To add concentric shapes, piece the top of the base (1A, 4A) of the ray first. (See page 51 and Piecing for Split-Star Variations, page 55.)

 Split rays can be stitched together before foundation piecing, but they must be oriented with the split seam on the foundation. See page 55 for more information.

Pattern 2

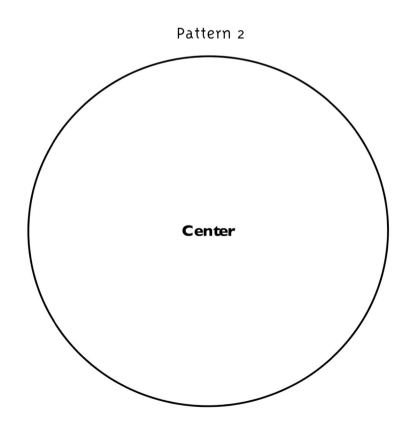

Center

FABRIC CUTTING PLANS

Refer to pages 50 and 52 to precut fabric into oversized shapes.

16-Point Starflower
#1A: Cut 8.
#1: Cut 8.
#2 and 3: Cut 16 total (background).
#4: Cut 8.
#5: Cut 8.
Center circle: Cut 1.

32-Point Starflower
#1A: Cut 16.
#1: Cut 16.
#2 and 3: Cut 32 total (background).
#4A: Cut 8.
#4: Cut 8.
#5: Cut 8.
#6: Cut 8.
Center circle: Cut 1.

16-Point Swirling Star
#1: Cut 8; split.
#2 and 3: Cut 16 total (background).
#4/5: Cut 8; split.
Center circle: Cut 1.

32-Point Swirling Star
#1A: Cut 16.
#1: Cut 16.
#2 and 3: Cut 32 total (background).
#4: Cut 8; split.
#5/6: Cut 8; split.

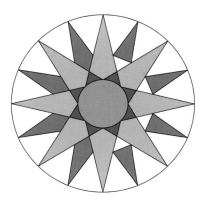

16- point Starflower/half concentric

16-point Starflower piecing sequence

32-point Starflower/half concentric

32-point Starflower piecing sequence

16-point Swirling Star/half concentric

16-point Swirling Star piecing sequence

32-point Swirling Star

32-point Swirling Star piecing sequence

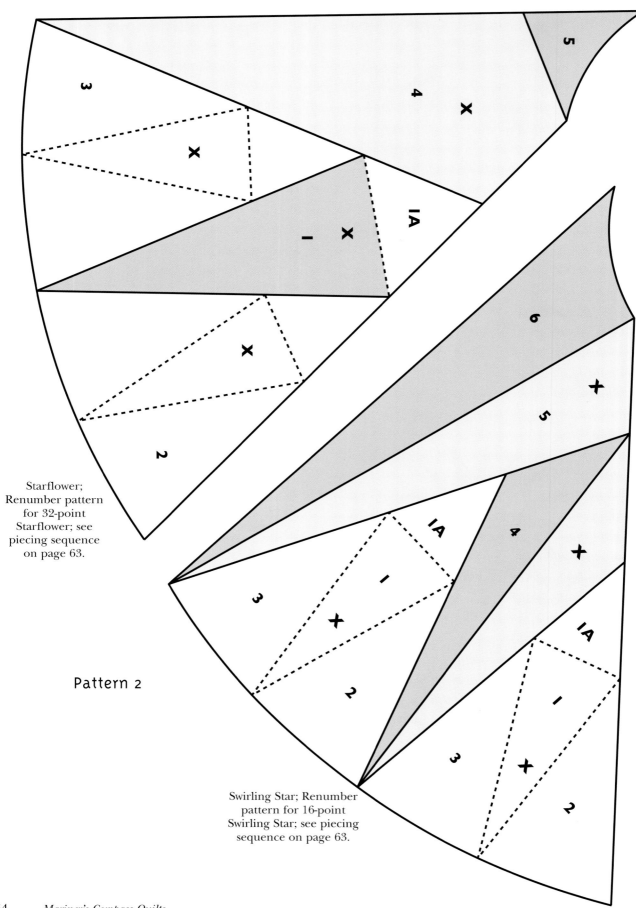

Starflower;
Renumber pattern
for 32-point
Starflower; see
piecing sequence
on page 63.

Pattern 2

Swirling Star; Renumber
pattern for 16-point
Swirling Star; see piecing
sequence on page 63.

This star is very splashy if you use high-contrast fabrics in the split. You get the most drama if you use the fabrics with the most contrast where they meet in the center of the star.

This star is the same size as the Basic Mariner's Compass star (page 62) and can be used with the outer ring patterns (page 67). The expanding checkerboard background pattern (page 70) can be used for the background square.

TIP Sew the #1 dark and light pieces together, then press the seam allowances open. This will help give the tips of #1 evenly split points. Press the seam allowances between the segments open to ensure matching at the intersections.

FABRIC CUTTING PLAN

Refer to pages 50 and 52 to precut fabric into oversized shapes.

#1: Cut 8; split (dark and light).
#2 and 3: Cut 16 total (background).
#4: Cut 4 each dark and light.*
#5: Cut 4 each dark and light.*
* Cut as mirror images.

Save the Whales, 34" x 34", by the author, 2004

16-point Split Star

Piecing sequence

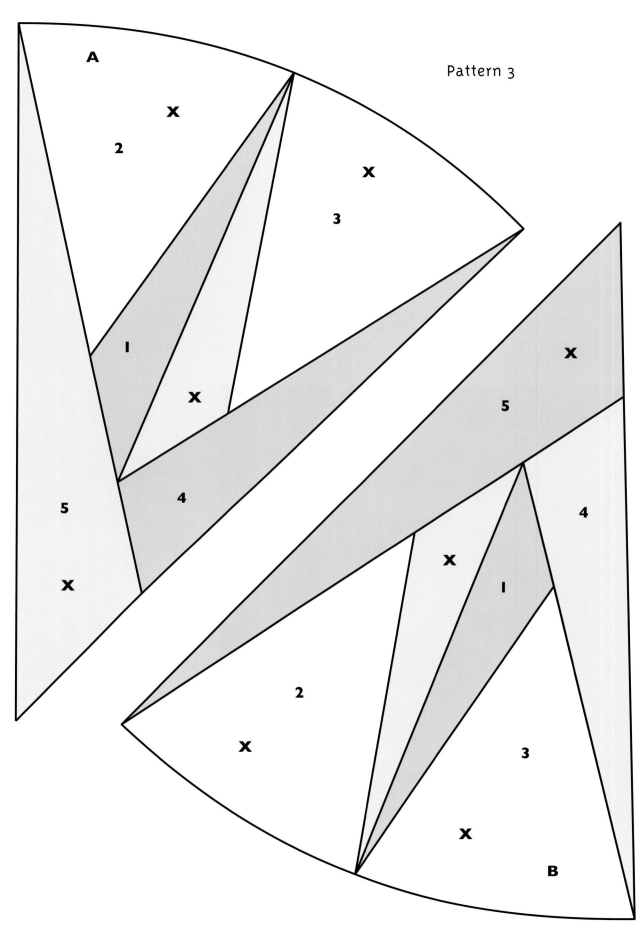

Pattern 3

PATTERN 4: Circling Geese and Outer Ring of Points (for 15″ Diameter Stars)

Circling geese add motion to the star to complete the design. Outer rings of points extend the star and make it appear more complex.

You can see quilt examples of the basic star with circling geese in *Yellow Marbled Star* (below), *Directional Interpretation* (page 37), *Heron's Way* (page 7), and *Malachite Star* (page 18). Outer rings of points appear in *Hawaii Star* (page 68) and *French Starflowers* (page 22).

Make eight copies of each foundation segment and follow the numbering sequence to cover the freezer-paper foundations. After all of the foundations are pieced, sew them into a ring and then piece them to the star circle.

FABRIC CUTTING PLANS

Refer to pages 50 and 52 to precut fabric into oversized shapes.

Circling Geese
A: Cut 32 (geese).
B and C: Cut 32 each (background).

Outer Rings of Points
A: Cut 32 (points).
B: Cut 32 (background).

Yellow Marbled Star, 26″ x 26″, by the author, 2004

Circling geese

Outer ring of points

Hawaii Star, 30" x 34", by the author, 2004

Pattern 4

These patterns fit the stars in Pattern 2 (page 62) and Pattern 3 (page 65).

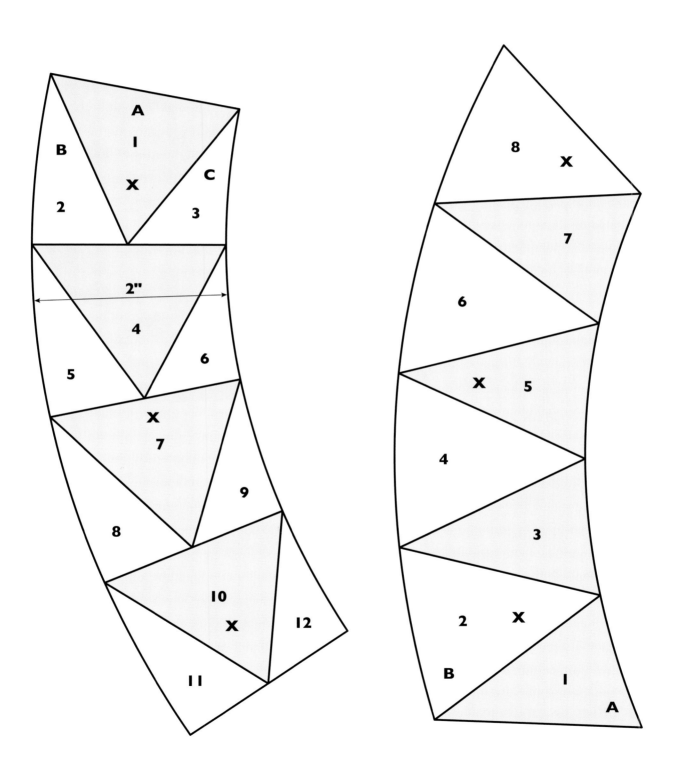

Chocolate Swirl, 36" x 36", by the author, 2004

The checkerboard lines follow the radiating lines of the star. The pattern can be used as a simple checkerboard background, or the innermost ring can be removed and replaced by circling geese or an outer ring of points. See *Mariner's Surround* (page 39) for an example of the latter. Illustrated variations can be seen in Chapter 2, page 40.

You can follow a number of possible color or value plans. The simplest approach is to make all the wedges using just two fabrics (one dark and one light value) or to keep the lights consistent and use a random plan for the darks, as I did in *Chocolate Swirl* (right). A more complex plan would be to make each expanding circle from a different fabric. In *Marbled Star* (page 41), for example, the fabrics in the yellow background become darker as the design works out from the center.

You'll find the pattern on the pullout at the back of the book. Make four copies and four reverse copies by positioning four sheets of freezer paper shiny sides together with another four sheets of freezer paper. Tack the papers together with the pattern and perforate. Be sure to mark the alternating dark and light squares on both the pattern and the reverse pattern so the value flows around the star (page 38).

Change the straight lines on the pattern to a curved line when replacing the innermost ring with a ring of circling geese or points.

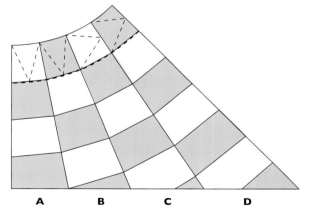

Piecing sequence

Cut the pattern into wedges A, B, C, and D. Cut 2½"-wide strips of your chosen fabric and alternately piece the light and dark fabrics to the wedges. When the wedges are all covered, trim and piece them back together in the original order.

These stars are similar to the basic stars in Pattern 2 (page 62) and Pattern 3 (page 65), but the length of the points varies within the star circle. For an example, see *Kyoto Stars* (page 89).

 TIP Be sure to cut a complete triangle of fabric when cutting background pieces #2 and #3 to avoid problems with print fabrics.

FABRIC CUTTING PLANS

Refer to pages 50 and 52 to precut fabric into oversized shapes.

Swirling Star
#1: Cut 8; split.
#2 and 3: Cut 16 total (background). See tip.
#4/5: Cut 8; split.
Center circle: Cut 1.

Starflower
#1A: Cut 8.
#1: Cut 8.
#2 and 3: Cut 16 total (background). See tip.
#4: Cut 8.
#5: Cut 8.
Center circle: Cut 1.

Split Star
#1: Cut 8; split.
#2 and 3: Cut 16 total (background). See tip.
#4: Cut 4 each, light and dark.*
#5: Cut 4 each, light and dark.*
*Cut as mirror images.

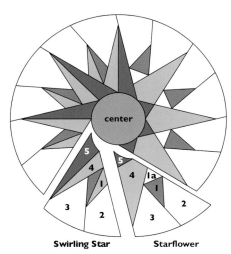

Swirling Star and Starflower
piecing sequence

Split Star piecing sequence

Detail of *Kyoto Stars*. See page 89 for a full view of this quilt.

Pattern 6

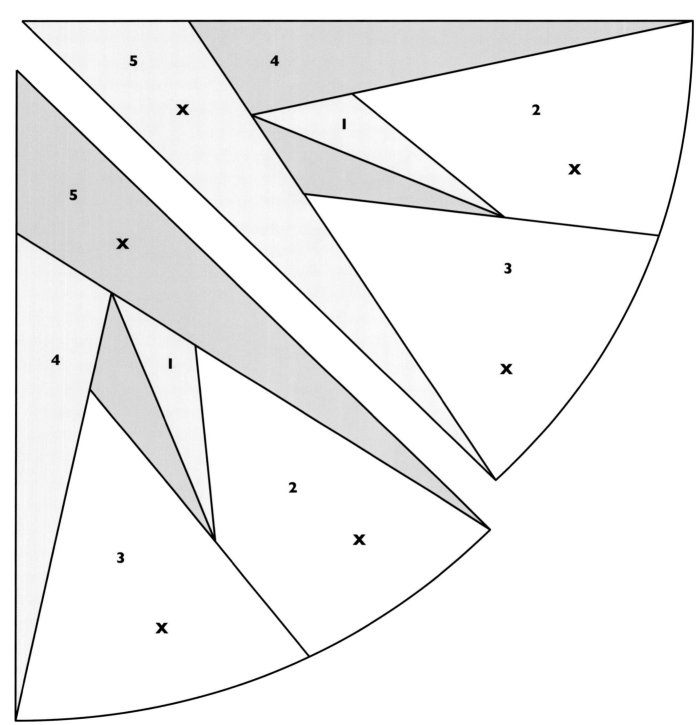

Rays of varying length Split Star

Pattern 6

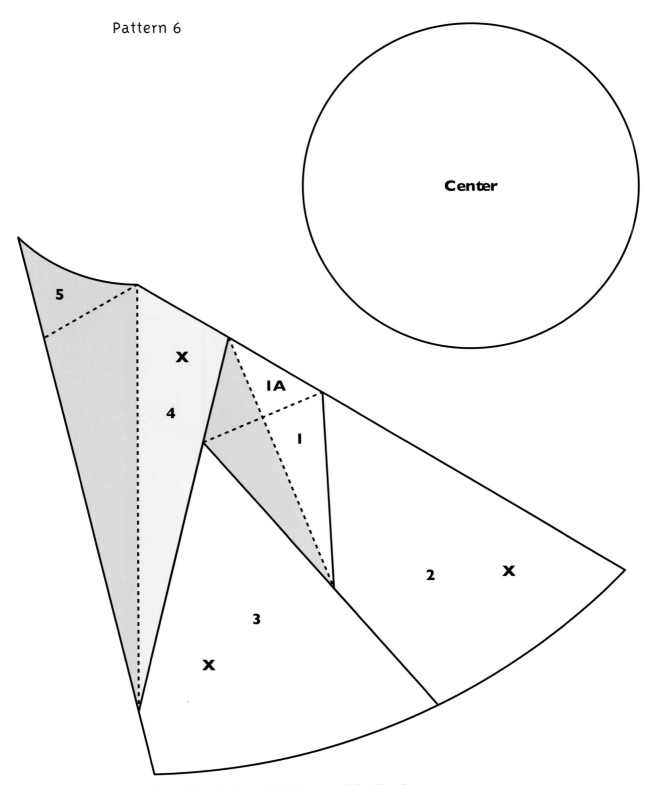

Rays of varying length Starflower and Swirling Star

I love the fleur-de-lis motif and have included three variations on page 75. The motif is commonly used to indicate north on the compass. Compass designs on maps often include the letters representing south, east, and west as well. A study of old maps or books about cartography will probably give you even more ideas for fleur-de-lis designs. You can use a photocopier to size the patterns to fit your quilt.

You can cut the fleur-de-lis shapes from a single fabric, as shown in *Daisy Star* (page 24), but cartographers often show them with light and dark sides and split center points. Cut the pattern pieces apart to make the templates. After appliquéing the other pieces in place, apply the horizontal bar joining the other pieces. You can position the motif at the top of the northern point as well as on the star. See *Save the Whales* (page 65). Use your preferred method for appliqué.

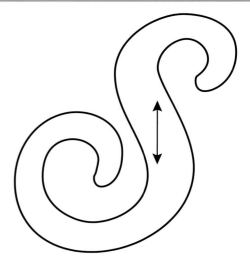

Star of Provence,
34" x 34", by the author, 1998. In the collection of Pat Scoville.

This is one of my favorite star patterns, but it is not a Mariner's Compass design as it has only 20 points. It has enough complexity to be more interesting than the basics stars, but it sews together easily. The patterns have been drafted so that the star points do not touch the outer circle but float ½" from it, which creates some space around the star. This makes it easier to piece—you don't need to get every point to end exactly on the outside star circles. Examples of this design include *Twilight Star With Circling Geese* (page 77), *Walking the Dog* (page 45), *Blooming Compass* (page 17), and the large top block on *New Directions* (page 22).

 TIP The arrows on the patterns refer to the preferred pressing direction of the seam allowances to help with matching intersections.

Circling Geese

Make eight copies of the patterns on page 78 for the 20" star, or twelve copies from page 79 for the 30" star, and piece following the sequence shown. Cut the appropriate number of geese and background triangles (40 for the 20" star and 60 for the 30" star). Sew the segments together and then piece the star to the ring of geese.

FABRIC CUTTING PLAN

Refer to pages 50 and 52 to precut fabric into oversized shapes.

Outside Star
#1, 2, 3, 4 (background), and 5 (background): Cut 20 of each piece from contrasting fabrics of alternating values. See tip, page 71.
Example: #1 dark, #2 light, #3 medium, #4 light (background), #5 light (background).

Inside Star
#1: Cut 5.
#2 and 3: Cut 10 total (background). See tip, page 71.
#4: Cut 5.
Center circle: Cut 1.

Twilight Star—inside star

Twilight Star—outside star

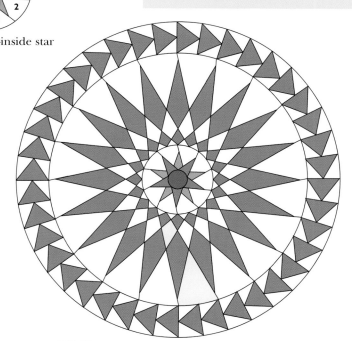

20" diameter Twilight Star with circling geese

Twilight Star With Circling Geese (quilt top), 35" x 35", by the author, 2003. Example of circling geese on 30" diameter star.

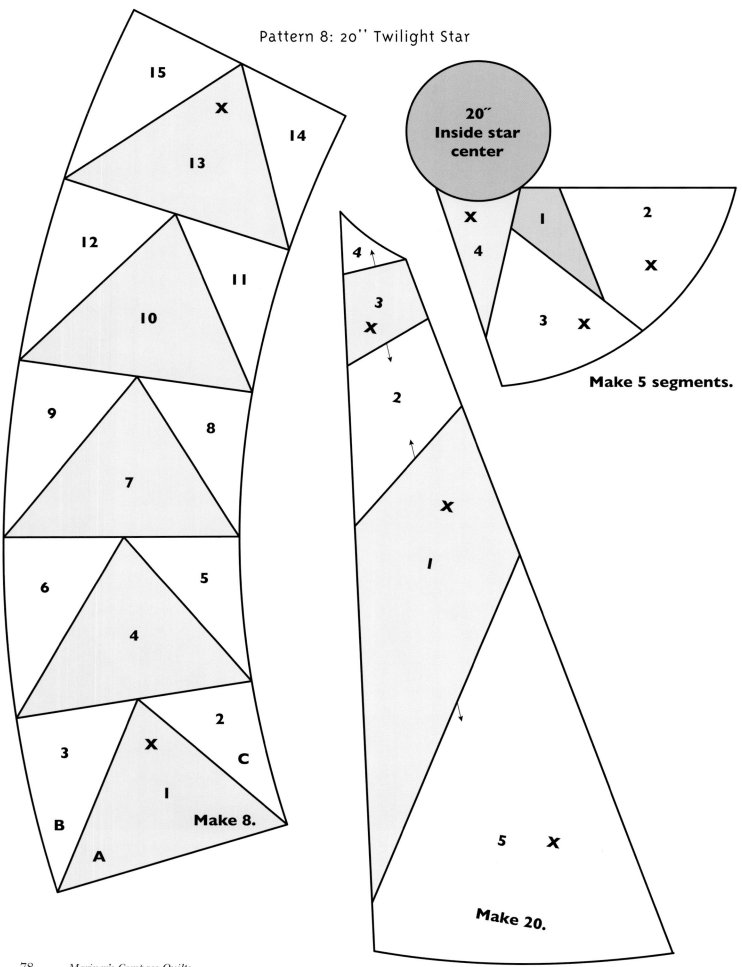

15

X

14

13

12

11

10

9

8

7

20''
Inside star
center

X

1

2

4

X

3

X

3

X

Make 5 segments.

4

3

X

2

X

1

5

4

6

3

2

C

X

1

B

A

Make 8.

5

X

Make 20.

Pattern 8: 30'' Twilight Star

You can find the pattern for the outside star ray on the pullout at the back of the book.

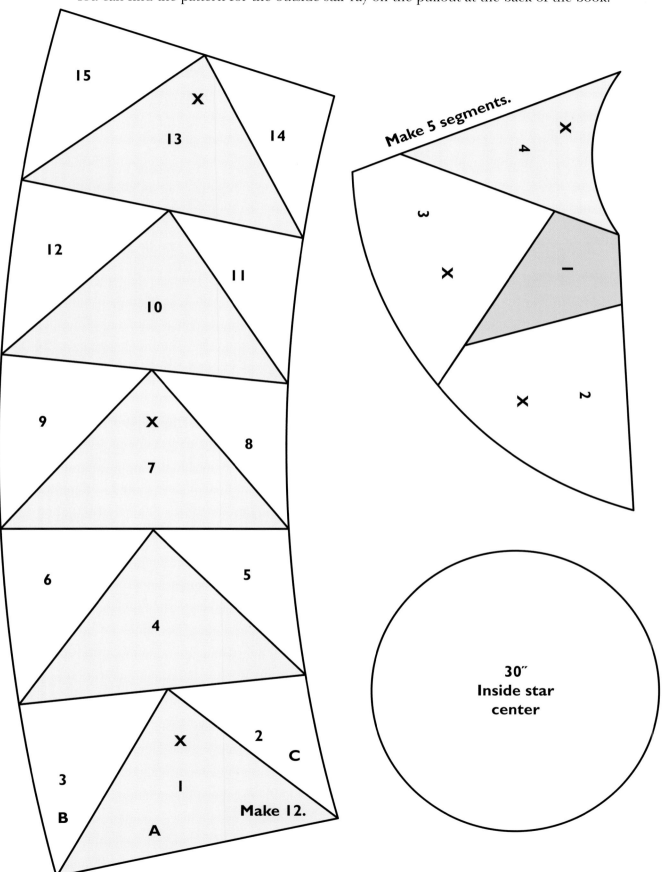

Make 5 segments.

Make 12.

30"
Inside star
center

Patterns 9 and 10 (page 82) are based on the folk-art designs of the farmers of Costa Rica. These farmers paint the huge mahogany wheels of their oxcarts, as well as the carts themselves, with elaborate designs (see page 10). You can see a version of this design with circling geese in *Amish Mariner's Compass* (page 30).

The outer star and middle star are pieced together following the general instructions (page 50). You can piece a third star in the center, or the center can be left as a circle of the background fabric. The middle and/or center stars can be added after the outer star is complete.

FABRIC CUTTING PLANS

Refer to pages 50 and 52 to precut fabric into oversized shapes.

Outside Star
Cut 18 of each piece (light and dark for the split rays).

Middle Star
Cut 18 of each piece.
Cut 1 center circle.
Or
Center Star
Cut 6 of each piece.
Cut 1 center circle.

Cartwheel Costa Rica, 43" x 43", by the author, 1994

Circling Geese Option

Make nine copies of the pattern on the pullout in the back of the book, and piece following the sequence on the pattern. Cut 40 geese and 40 of each background triangle. Sew the segments together, and then piece the star to the ring of geese.

The piecing can follow the regular numerical sequence, using strips of fabric to be cut and trimmed as you sew. Or you can sew light and dark strips together, press the seams open, and precut fabric patches for the stars using the presewn fabrics. You will need to match the centers of the dark/light fabrics with the center lines on the foundations. See page 51 and Piecing for Split-Star Variations (page 55) for additional guidance.

Pattern 9

You can find the pattern for the outside star ray on the pullout at the back of the book.

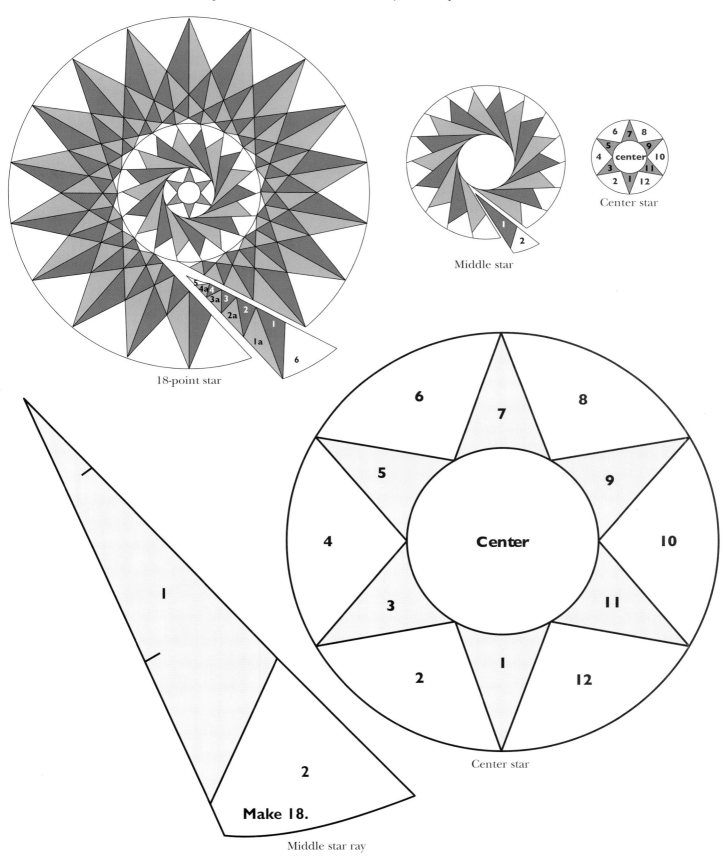

18-point star

Middle star

Center star

Make 18.

Middle star ray

Center star

This design is also based on the folk-art designs of the Costa Rican farmers. The outer star and the inner star are pieced following the general instructions (page 50).

Cartwheel Costa Rica 2 (block), 15" diameter, by the author, 2004

The piecing can follow the regular numerical sequence, using strips of fabric to be cut and trimmed as you sew. Or you can sew light and dark strips together, press the seams open, and precut fabric patches for the stars using the presewn fabrics. You will need to match the centers of the dark/light fabrics with the center lines on the foundations. See page 51 and Piecing for Split-Star Variations (page 55) for additional guidance.

FABRIC CUTTING PLAN

Refer to pages 50 and 52 to precut fabric into oversized shapes.

Outside Star
Cut 12 of each piece (light and dark for the split rays). I used 4 different pairs—2 in warm colors and 2 in cool colors.

Inside Star
Cut 6 of each piece (light and dark for the split rays). Cut 1 center circle.

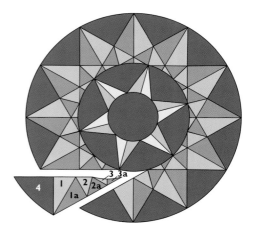

12-point star

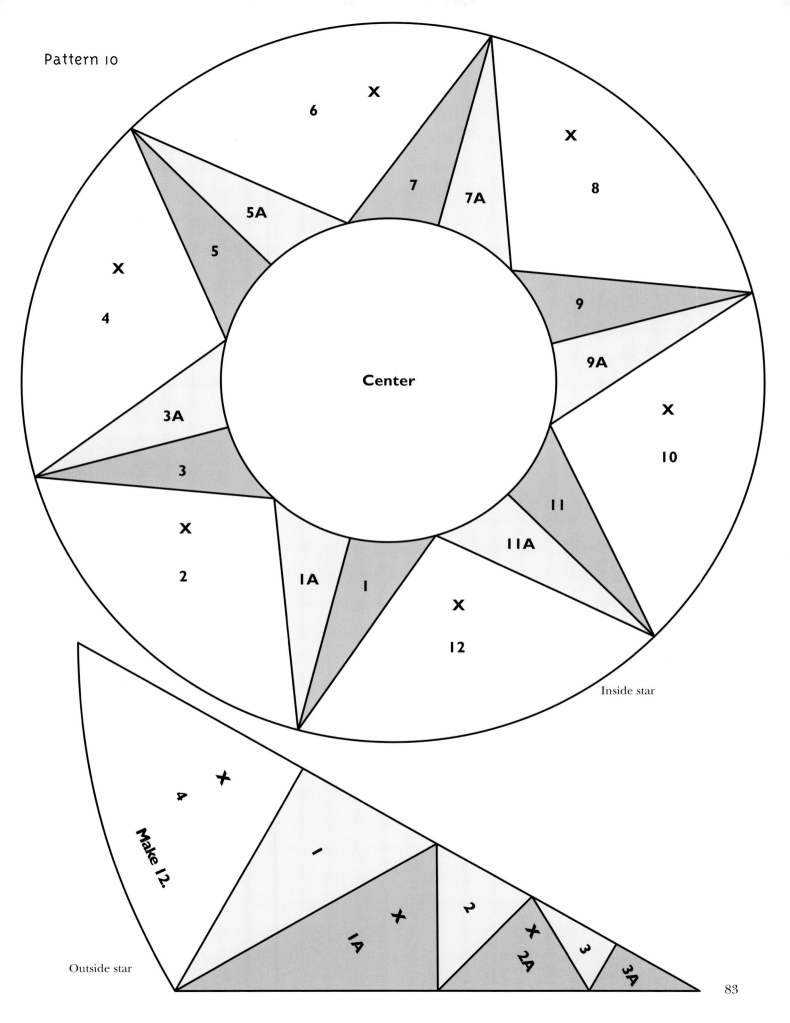

Pattern 10

Center

Inside star

Outside star

Make 12.

83

You will find these two patterns on the pullout at the back of the book. One pattern has a circle in the center and the other an oval. They can be used for 16-point or 32-point stars, with or without stars in the center. The patterns are offered as half a star. Make two foundation copies of each segment. Some of the foundation segments may be broken into smaller segments for piecing. Then piece the eight major segments back together before joining them in to the complete oval star.

FABRIC CUTTING PLANS

Refer to pages 50 and 52 to precut fabric into oversized shapes.

Outside Star
There are four different segment shapes in these designs, and each is used twice. Because of the complexity of the design, I have found it easiest to make an extra set of the four patterns. Cut them into individual templates to cut two of each shape.

Inside Circle/Oval Star
You can complete the star with a circle or oval of a single fabric or use a center star pattern. The round star has two different segments (A and B) used four times, and the oval star has four different segments (A, B, C, and D) used twice.

16-point oval star with round center

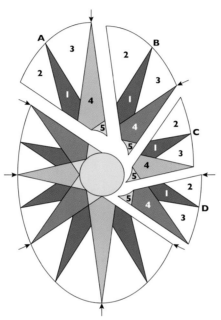

16-point oval star piecing sequence

32-point oval star with oval center

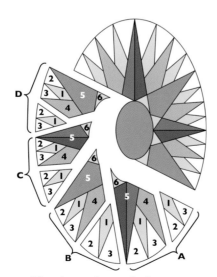

32-point oval star piecing sequence

This is a dramatic star with lots of energy. You can find an example of this star in *Pulsar* (page 92). You can find the pattern on the pullout at the back of the book. Examples of a slightly different 64-point star appear in *Rising Sun* (page 16) and *Starlight, Starbright* (below).

Because this star has so many points, the foundation must be broken into several segments for piecing. Then the 8 major segments are pieced back together before they are joined into the complete 64-point star. The design can be simplified by eliminating the concentric-circle variations or by eliminating the smallest set of points, creating a 32-point star.

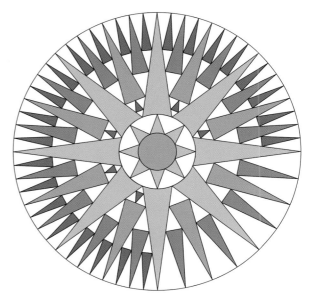

64-point star with 32-point variation

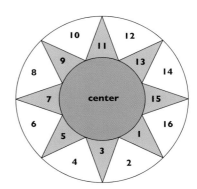

8-point star center;
pattern on page 60

Detail of *Starlight, Starbright* by Janyce Anderson. See page 44 for a full view of this quilt.

FABRIC CUTTING PLAN

Refer to pages 50 and 52 to precut fabric into oversized shapes.

64-Point Star

#1: Cut 32.
#2 and 3: Cut 64 total.
#4: Cut 32.
#5: Cut 16.
#6: Cut 16.
#7: Cut 8.
#8 and 9: Cut 16 total.
#10: Cut 8.
#11: Cut 8.
#12: Cut 8.

Assembly

1. Piece units A, B, D, and E.
2. Piece A to B and D to E.
3. Piece A/B to C.
4. Piece A/B/C to D/E.
5. Piece F (#12) to left side of A/B/C/D/E. Make 8.
6. Sew all A/B/C/D/E/F segments together to complete outer star.
7. Assemble 8-point center star (see Pattern 1, page 60) and appliqué to outer star.

FABRIC CUTTING PLAN

Refer to pages 50 and 52 to precut fabric into oversized shapes.

32-Point Star

#1A: Cut 16.
#1: Cut 16.
#2 and 3: Cut 32 total.
#4: Cut 8.
#5: Cut 8.
#6: Cut 8.

Assembly

1. Piece units A and B.
2. Assemble A, B, and C. Make 8.
3. Sew all A/B/C units together to complete outer star.
4. Assemble 8-point center star (see Pattern 1, page 60) and appliqué to outer star.

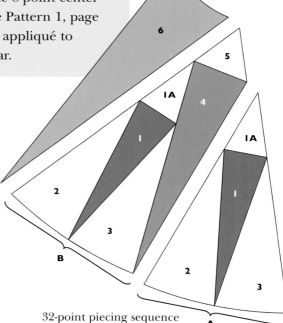

32-point piecing sequence

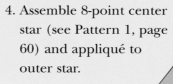

64-point piecing sequence

Square Blocks

Add ¼"-wide seam allowances to the background block patterns on the pullout at the back of the book. Cut four of each. Background blocks are 2" larger than the diameter of the star (except for 30" stars and ovals). They can be made smaller or larger by increasing or decreasing the outside edges.

1. 8" diameter; 10" block. Use with 8-point star.

2. 14" diameter; 16" block. Use with 16-point star with rays of varying lengths (e.g., *Kyoto Stars*, page 89).

3. 15" diameter; 17" block. Use with Basic Mariner's Compass, Starflower, Swirling Star, Split Star, and Cartwheel Costa Rica 2.

4. 19" diameter; 21" block. Use with outer ring and circling geese.

5. 20" diameter; 22" block. Use with Twilight Star.

6. 25" diameter; 27" block. Use with 20" Twilight Star with geese.

7. 30" diameter; 34" block. Use with 30" Twilight Star, Cartwheel Costa Rica, and 64-Point Star (e.g., *Pulsar*, page 92).

8. 36" diameter; 38" block. Use with 30" Twilight Star with geese and Cartwheel Costa Rica with geese.

Detail of ***The Stars Are Smiling at You***. See page 32 for a full view of this quilt.

Rectangular (Oval) Blocks

The same 18" x 27" block background pattern on the pullout can be used for both oval star patterns.

Detail of ***New Directions***. See page 22 for a full view of this quilt.

The Projects

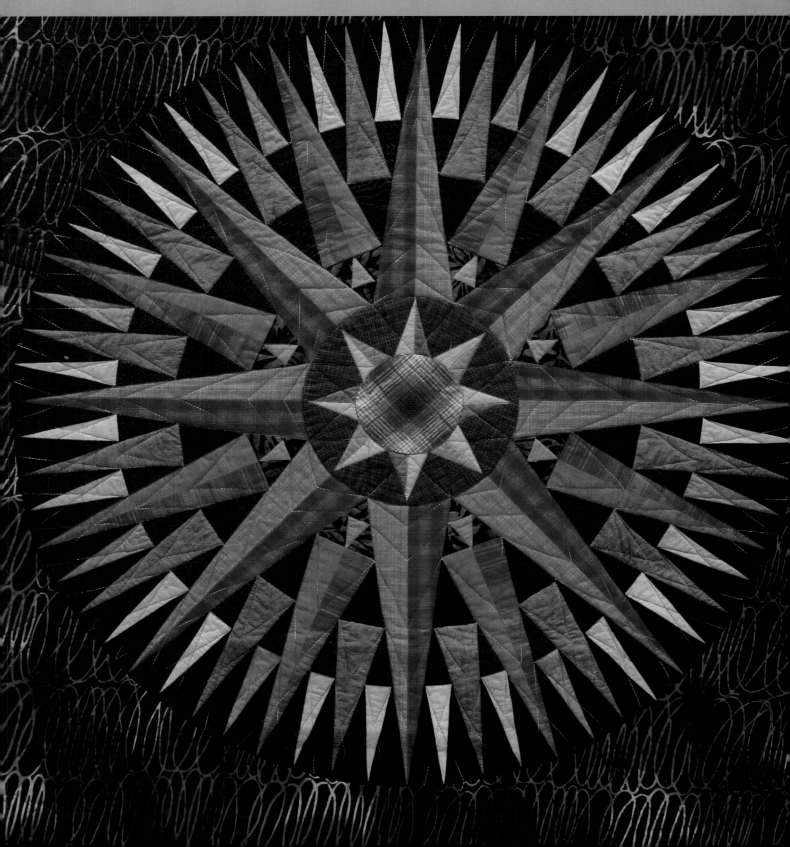

Kyoto Stars

Finished Quilt: 83" x 83"
Finished Block: 16"

Japanese textiles, both vintage and reproduction, were used in this quilt. You can use any fabrics you like, but select fabrics with relatively small-scale prints for the stars and larger-scale prints for the background squares. I chose dark chambray fabrics for the star circles because these fabrics have a substantial feel that contrasts well with the stars. The sashings are all woven stripes cut across the length. I made the Pinwheel blocks in the intersections with high-contrast fabrics to balance the sparkly stars, and I cut the inner border from checkerboard fabric. The outer border is also a larger-scale print.

Kyoto Stars, 83" x 83", by the author, 2004

Materials

Stars and star centers:

3¾ yards *total* of a variety of fabrics in light to medium values to contrast with star backgrounds

Star circle backgrounds:

2½ yards *total* of fabric in dark value to contrast with stars

Star block background squares:

2½ yards *total* of fabric in medium value to contrast with star circle backgrounds and sashing*
*1½ yards if using Pattern 13

Pinwheels:

⅝ yard *each* of fabric in light and dark value

Sashing:

2½ yards *total* of striped fabrics in medium or dark value to contrast with background blocks

Inner border:

⅓ yard of fabric in light value to contrast with sashing and outer border

Outer border:

2½ yards of fabric in medium value to contrast with inner border

Binding:

⅝ yard

Backing:

7¼ yards

Batting:

87" x 87"

Cutting

Star block backgrounds:

Cut 36 of Pattern 13 for 14" diameter, 16" finished block on the pullout, or 9 squares 16½" x 16½".

Pinwheels:

Cut 32 squares 3⅞" x 3⅞" from each fabric (64 squares total).

Sashing:

Cut 24 strips 6½" x 16½".

Inner border:

Cut 8 strips 1" x width of fabric. Piece as necessary, then cut 2 strips 72½" long and 2 strips 73½" long.

Outer border:

Cut 2 strips 5½" x 73½" and 2 strips 5½" x 83½" along the lengthwise grain (parallel to the selvage).

Binding:

Cut 9 strips 2" x fabric width.

Making the Stars

1. Refer to pages 50–55 for guidance, and prepare foundations for 9 Pattern 6 stars: 4 Starflowers (page 73), 4 Swirling Stars (page 73), and 1 Split Star (page 72).

Detail of Starflower from *Kyoto Stars*

Detail of Swirling Star from *Kyoto Stars*

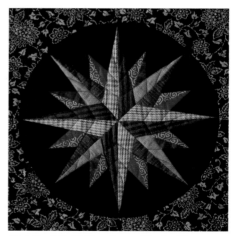

Detail of Split Star from *Kyoto Stars*

2. Refer to pages 55–57 and follow the instructions for piecing stars into circles and inserting the star circles into the 16½" background squares.

Making the Pinwheels

1. Draw a diagonal line from corner to corner on the wrong side of each 3⅞" square of light fabric. Place each marked square right sides together with a 3⅞" square of dark fabric. Stitch ¼" from the diagonal line on both sides.

2. Cut on the marked diagonal line to create 2 half-square-triangle units. Press the seams toward the dark fabric. Make 64.

Make 64.

3. Arrange and stitch 4 units from Step 2 to create a pinwheel as shown. Press. Make 16. Notice that the pinwheels can rotate in either direction.

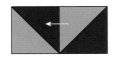

Make 16.

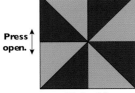

Pinwheel rotation option

Assembly

1. Sew the Star blocks, Pinwheel blocks, and sashing strips in rows as shown. Press. Sew the rows together. Press.

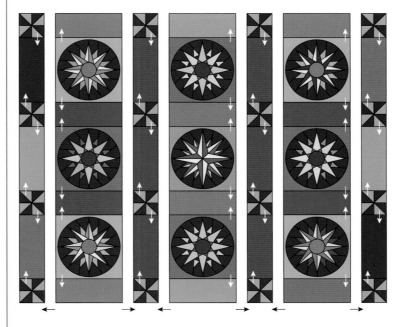

2. Sew the inner border and then the outer border to the quilt as shown. Press the seams toward each newly added border.

3. Press the quilt top. Prepare the backing and layer the backing, batting, and quilt top. Baste the layers. Quilt as desired and bind the quilt edges.

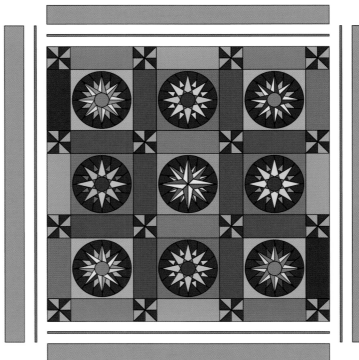

Pulsar

Finished Quilt: 46" x 46"

This quilt features the 30" diameter 64-point star with a 6"-wide border.

I chose to use warm and cool colors against a dark background, and the selection of complementary colors (opposite colors on the color wheel) makes the design appear to pulse. The star fabrics are various shades of bright solids and plaids. The backgrounds of the star circle are various darks, and the background of the square is a black print. The border combines a solid black background with geese in the same brightly colored solid fabrics as the star.

Pulsar With Drifting Geese Border, 46" x 46", by the author, 2004

Materials

Star:

¼ yard *each* of 10 different brightly colored solids and plaids

Star circle background:

1¼ yards *total* of fabric in dark values

Star block background square:

1 yard of fabric in dark value

Drifting geese border background:

1⅜ yards of fabric in dark value

Drifting geese border triangles:

¾ yard *total* of 8 different brightly colored fabrics

Binding:

⅜ yard

Backing:

2⅞ yards

Batting:

50" x 50"

Cutting

Star block backgrounds:

Cut 4 of Pattern 13 for 30" diameter, 34" block on the pullout, or 1 square 34½" x 34½".

Drifting geese border background:

Cut 21 strips 2" x fabric width; crosscut into
92* squares 2" x 2" (A),
80* rectangles 2" x 3½" (B), and
72* rectangles 2" x 5" (C).
*Includes extra squares and rectangles; see tip.

Drifting geese border triangles:

Cut a *total* of 118* rectangles 2" x 3½" (D).
*Includes extra rectangles; see tip.

Binding:

Cut 5 strips 2" x fabric width.

I cut and made extra brightly colored and background units for the border so I could control the color arrangement as I went along.

Making the Star

1. Refer to pages 50–55 for guidance, and prepare foundations for the 30" diameter star and the 8" diameter star center. Pattern 12, the 64-point 30" diameter star, is on the pullout. Use Pattern 1 (page 60) for the 8" star center.

2. Refer to page 57 and follow the instructions for inserting the completed star circle into the 34½" background square.

Making the Drifting Geese Border

Follow these steps and use the drifting geese rectangles and squares to create the six different units shown.

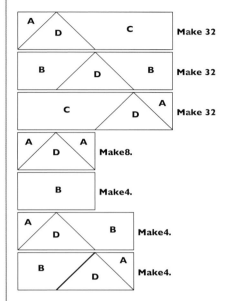

1. Place a 2" x 3½" brightly colored rectangle and a background piece right sides together as shown. Stitch on the diagonal from corner to corner. Trim and press.

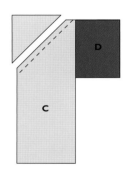

2. Repeat to sew another background piece to the opposite end of the unit from Step 1 as shown.

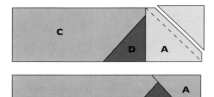

3. Repeat Steps 1 and 2 to make the required number of each of the 6 units.

Assembly

1. Arrange and sew the drifting geese units as shown or in any similar arrangement. Press. Make 4 borders and 4 corner units.

2. Sew the borders and corner units to the center star block as shown. Press.

3. Press the quilt top. Prepare the backing and layer the backing, batting, and quilt top. Baste the layers. Quilt as desired and bind the quilt edges.

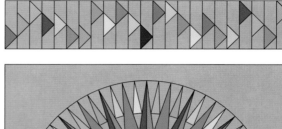
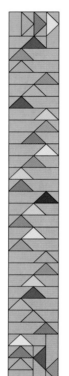 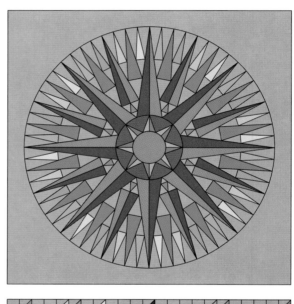 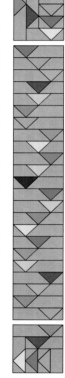

Bibliography

Anderson, Alex. *Paper Piecing With Alex Anderson.* Lafayette, CA: C&T Publishing, 2002.

Collins, Sally. *Borders, Bindings & Edges: The Art of Finishing Your Quilt.* Lafayette, CA: C&T Publishing, 2004.

Doak, Carol. *40 Bright & Bold Paper-Pieced Blocks: 12-Inch Designs From Carol Doak.* Woodinville, WA: Martingale & Company, 2002.

Faoro, Victoria, ed. *Mariner's Compass Quilts: New Quilts From an Old Favorite.* Paducah, KY: American Quilter's Society, 1997.

Garber, Gail. *Stellar Journeys: Flying Geese & Star Quilts.* Paducah, KY: American Quilter's Society, 2001.

Hargrave, Harriett, and Sharyn Craig. *The Art of Classic Quiltmaking.* Lafayette, CA: C&T Publishing, 2000.

Mathieson, Judy. *Block Factory: Mariner's Compass Edition.* CD-ROM. Quilt-Pro Systems in association with C&T Publishing, 1987.

_____. *Mariner's Compass: An American Quilt Classic.* Lafayette, CA: C&T Publishing, 1987.

_____. *Mariner's Compass Quilts: New Directions.* Lafayette, CA: C&T Publishing, 1995.

Porter, Christine. *Quilt Designs From Decorative Floor Tiles.* Newton Abbot, UK: David & Charles Books, 2003.

About the Author

JUDY MATHIESON has always loved fabric and made most of her own clothes while growing up. She became interested in quiltmaking while completing her degree in home economics at California State University, Northridge. She has been teaching since 1977 and is certified by the National Quilt Association as a judge. She lectures and conducts workshops throughout the United States and internationally for quilt guilds and conferences. Her prize-winning work appears regularly in national juried shows and quilt publications. She is proud that her quilt *Nautical Stars* (page 46) was included in the exhibit 100 Best Quilts of the Twentieth Century. Mariner's Compass is her favorite quilt pattern, and she has published two previous books and a CD-ROM on the subject.

Judy lived for over 30 years in California's San Fernando Valley but returned to Northern California in 1996. She lives in rural Sebastopol with her husband, Jack, and three very important Border Collies. Their two sons live nearby.

Judy can be reached at www.JudyMathieson.com.

For more information, ask for a free catalog:
C&T Publishing, Inc.
P.O. Box 1456
Lafayette, CA 94549
(800) 284-1114
Email: ctinfo@ctpub.com
Website: www.ctpub.com

For hand-marbled fabrics (page 18):
Marjorie Lee Bevis
1401 Oakwood Drive
Oakland, OR 97462
(541)459-1921
(541)459-1931 (fax)
Website: www.marbledfabrics.com

For quilting supplies:
Cotton Patch Mail Order
3405 Hall Lane, Dept. CTB
Lafayette, CA 94549
(800) 835-4418
(925) 283-7883
Email: quiltusa@yahoo.com
Website: www.quiltusa.com

NOTE: Fabrics used in the quilts shown may not be currently available as fabric manufacturers keep most fabrics in print for only a short time.

Index